# ROOF & SIDING
## ESSENTIALS

QUICK
STEPS™

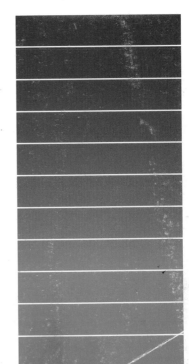

COWLES
Creative Publishing

A Division of Cowles Enthusiast Media, Inc.

# Credits

Copyright © 1997
Cowles Creative Publishing, Inc.
Formerly Cy DeCosse Incorporated
5900 Green Oak Drive
Minnetonka, Minnesota 55343
1-800-328-3895
All rights reserved
Printed in U.S.A.

COWLES
Creative Publishing
*A Division of Cowles Enthusiast Media, Inc.*

*President/COO:* Nino Tarantino
*Executive V.P./Editor-in-Chief:* William B. Jones

*Created by:* The Editors of Cowles Creative Publishing, Inc.,
in cooperation with Black & Decker.  is
a trademark of the Black & Decker Corporation and is
used under license.

*Printed on American paper by:*
 Quebecor Printing
 99 98 97 96 / 5 4 3 2 1

COWLES
Enthusiast Media

*President/COO:* Philip L. Penny

## Books available in this series:

6015574457

## NOTICE TO READERS

# Contents

# Replacing & Repairing Roof Systems

The roof system has a greater exposure to the elements than any other part of your house. As a result, it requires the most attention and the most frequent maintenance. This is especially true because problems in the roof system, like leaks or blocked ventilation, lead quickly to damage in other parts of your house.

A roof system is composed of several elements that work together to provide three basic and essential functions for your home: shelter, drainage, and ventilation. The roof covering and the flashing shed water, directing it to the gutters and downspouts to channel it away from the foundation of your house. Air intake and outtake vents keep fresh air circulating below the roof sheathing, preventing moisture buildup and overheating.

Roof system projects range in complexity, from simply caulking a small hole in a shingle, to removing and replacing shingles, building paper, flashing, and sheathing. Whatever the complex-ity of the repairs your roof system requires, it is very important that you have a thorough under-standing of how all the elements of the system work. By understanding your roof system and making timely repairs, you can ensure that your roof system performs for its full, useful life span.

This sections shows:

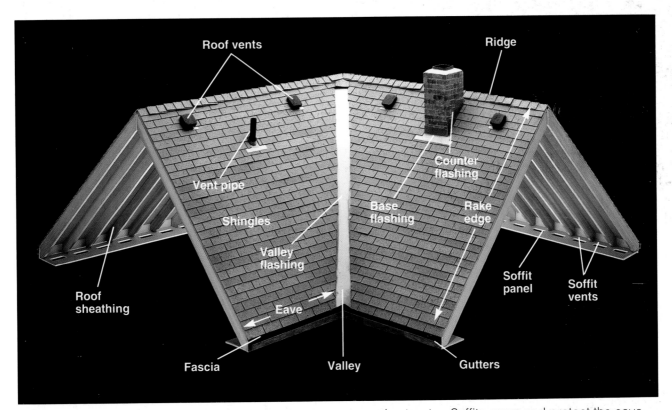

**The elements of a roof system** work together to provide shelter, drainage, and ventilation. The roof covering is composed of sheathing, building paper, and shingles. Metal flashing is attached in valleys and around chimneys, vent pipes, and other roof elements to seal out water. Soffits cover and protect the eave area below the roof overhang. Fascia, usually attached at the ends of the rafters, supports soffit panels as well as a gutter and downspout system. Soffit vents and roof vents keep fresh air flowing under the roof.

# Working Safely

By taking common-sense precautions you can work just as safely outdoors as indoors—even though the exterior presents a few additional safety considerations.

Since many exterior repairs require you to work at heights, learning and following the basic rules of safe ladder and scaffolding use is very important (pages 8 to 9). And any time you are working outside, the weather should play a key role in just about every aspect of how you conduct your work: from the work clothes you select, to the amount of work you decide to undertake.

In addition to the information shown on the following pages, here are some important safety precautions to follow when working outdoors:

• When possible, work with a helper in case there is an emergency. If you have to work alone, inform a friend or family member so they can check on you periodically. If you own a portable telephone, keep it handy at all times.
• Never work at heights, or with tools, if you have consumed alcohol or medication.
• Do not work outdoors in stormy weather. Do not work at heights when it is windy.

## Tip for Working Safely

**Set up your work site for quick disposal** of waste materials. Old nails, jagged metal from flashing, and piles of old shingles all are safety hazards when left on the ground. Use a wheelbarrow to transfer waste to a dumpster or trash can immediately. NOTE: Disposal of building materials is regulated in most areas. Check with your local waste management department.

**Wear sensible clothing and protective equipment** when working outdoors, including: a cap to protect against direct sunlight, eye protection when working with tools or chemicals, a particle mask when sanding, work gloves, full-length pants, and a long-sleeved shirt. A tool organizer turns a 5-gallon bucket into a safe and convenient container for transporting tools.

# Tips for Working Safely

**Permanently attach a fastener** to the top of your ladder for tying off power cords or air hoses. The weight of a power cord or hose is enough to drag most power tools off the roof. Drill a hole in the ladder and secure a cap bolt (above) to the ladder with a nut and bolt. Do not tie knots in cords and hoses.

**Create a storage surface** for tools. A sheet of plywood on top of a pair of sawhorses keeps tools off the ground, where they are a safety hazard (and where they can become damaged by moisture). A storage surface also makes it easy to locate tools when you need them.

**Stay clear of power cables.** Household service cables carry 100 amps of electricity or more. If you must work near a cable, use extreme caution, and use fiberglass or wood ladders only—never use metal ladders near cables.

**Use a GFCI extension cord** when working outdoors. GFCIs (Ground Fault Circuit Interrupters) shut off power if a short circuit occurs (often from contact with water).

**Use cordless tools** whenever possible to make your work easier and safer. Power cords, even when properly secured, are a nuisance and create many hazards, including tripping and tangling.

## Options for Working at Heights

**Use an extension ladder** for making quick repairs to gutters, fascia, and soffits, and to gain access to roofs. For larger projects, like painting walls, relying solely on ladders is inefficient and dangerous.

**Use scaffolding** for projects that require you to work at heights for extended periods of time, like preparing walls for paint. If you rent scaffolding, be sure to get assembly-and-use instructions from the rental center.

## Tips for Using Ladders and Scaffolds

**Provide level, stable footing** for ladders and scaffolding. Install sturdy blocking under the legs of ladders (left) if the ground is uneven, soft, or slippery, and always drive a stake n_____ ladder foot to keep the ladder from slipp_____ m the house.

Also insert sturdy blocking under scaffold feet (right) if the ground is soft or uneven. Add more blocking under legs in sloped areas, and use the adjustable leg posts for final leveling. If the scaffold has wheels, lock them securely with the hand brakes.

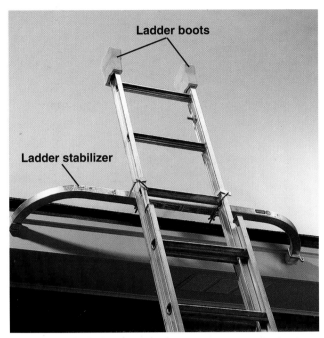

Attach an adjustable ladder stabilizer to your ladder to minimize the chance of slipping. Rest the feet of the stabilizer against broad, flat, stable surfaces only. In addition to making the ladder safer, a stabilizer allows you to work on areas directly in front of the ladder. If you do not use a stabilizer, cover the top ends of the ladder with ladder boots to prevent slipping and protect siding from scratches and dents.

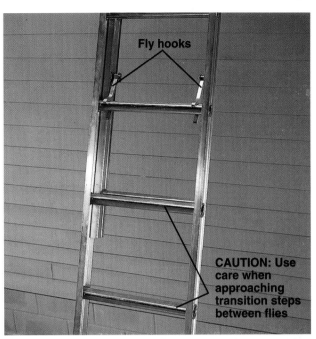

Make sure fly hooks are secure before climbing an extension ladder. The open ends of the hooks should grip a rung on the lower fly extension. Use extra caution when climbing past the fly hooks as you ascend and descend the ladder, and be aware of the points at each fly extension where the doubled rungs end, and single rungs begin.

Anchor ladders and scaffolding by tying them to a secure area, like a chimney—especially if you are not using a ladder stabilizer. If no sturdy anchoring spot exists, create one by driving a #10 screw eye into the fascia. When finished with the ladder, remove the screw eye and cover the hole with caulk.

## Ladder Safety Tips:

• Watch out for wires, branches, and overhangs when carrying ladders.

• Position extension ladders so the flat tops of the D-shaped rungs are facing up, parallel to the ground.

• Extend the ladder three feet above the roof edge for greater stability and to provide a gripping point when you mount or dismount the ladder (do not grip too aggressively).

• Do not exceed the work-load rating for your ladder. Limits are listed on the label of any ladder. Read all the safety recommendations.

• Climb on or off a ladder at a point as close to the ground as possible. Move steadily and keep your center of gravity low when crossing between the roof and the ladder.

• Never carry heavy items, like shingle bundles, up an extension ladder. Use a hoist (a simple cord and bucket will do), and pull the items up while you are standing securely on the roof. Lower the items down using the same method as well.

# Evaluating Roof Systems

**Shown cutaway for clarity**

Regular inspections are essential to maintaining a healthy roof system—more can go wrong in the roof area than in just about any other part of your house. Most roof damage is caused by water, either from precipitation or condensation below the roof materials. Because a failed shingle could be caused by a leak somewhere else in the roof, or by inadequate attic ventilation that results in condensation, simply replacing the shingle will not correct the leak. Make sure you eliminate any moisture source outside the damaged area before you repair the damage.

**Ice dams** occur when melting snow refreezes near the eaves, causing ice to back up under the shingles, where it melts onto the sheathing. To solve the problem, improve roof ventilation (pages 44 to 47).

## Finding & Evaluating Roof Leaks

**Inspect from inside your attic.** Look for discoloration, streaking, or rot on roof sheathing and rafters. Find the highest point of discoloration to pinpoint the source of the leak. Then, measure from the high point to roof vents, chimneys, or other roof elements so you can use their relative locations to help find the leak on the exterior of the roof. If the damage is minimal (left), and no rot has set in, simply repair shingles or flashing (pages 30 to 33). If there is substantial rot (right), tear off the shingles above the rot, replace damaged sheathing (page 17), and reshingle (pages 18 to 28). Fix any moisture problems outside the damaged area.

## Common Shingle Problems

**Buckled shingles** (top) and **cupped shingles** (bottom) usually are caused by lingering moisture beneath the shingle. Likely sources include condensation from poor attic ventilation (pages 44 to 47), or leaky shingles or flashing. If you find and fix the moisture problem, buckled shingles may flatten out by themselves. If they do not flatten out, replace them. Cupped shingles almost always require replacement. See pages 16 to 28 for major damage, or pages 30 to 31 for isolated damage. Do not install new shingles over cupped or buckled shingles.

**Damaged shingles** (top) and **worn shingles** (bottom) become increasingly common as a roof ages. Damage can occur on any roof, new or old, but it becomes more likely as the shingles age and the protective mineral surfaces wear down. Treat isolated damage or wear by replacing only the problem shingles (pages 30 to 33). Widespread damage and pervasive wear usually require that all the shingles be replaced, either by tearing off and reshingling (pages 16 to 28), or by installing new shingles over the old shingles (page 29—check building codes first).

## Gutter Problems

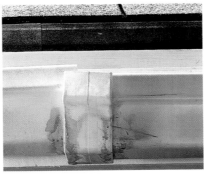

**Sagging gutters** can be caused by deteriorated fascia or by weight from a blockage. Remove the blockage, replace damaged fascia (page 35), then raise and refasten gutters (page 38).

**Leaking gutters** usually result from holes or separated joints (shown). Disassemble leaky joints, then caulk and reassemble the joint (page 40). Patch holes (pages 39 to 40).

**Damaged gutter sections** should be patched (pages 39 to 40) or replaced (page 41). If damage is widespread, replace with a new gutter system (pages 42 to 43).

## Flashing Problems

**Loose flashing** can be caused by external forces, like high wind, or by failure of sealant or fasteners. To repair, pull back the flashing enough to clean out the old sealant, and resecure with fresh roofing cement and new fasteners (page 30).

**Damaged and deteriorated flashing** are primary causes of roof leaks. Remove and replace the damaged piece (page 32). If several pieces are damaged or showing signs of wear, remove and replace all the flashing around the affected roof element (page 33).

## Fascia & Soffit Problems

**Pest damage and rot** are the primary enemies of soffits. Small spots of damage can be repaired by replacing the material (pages 36 to 37). If damage is more widespread, or if your house does not have soffits, and birds or insects are nesting in your eaves, install a new soffit system (page 34).

**Rotten fascia** is easy to spot from the ground on homes with no gutter system. If your house has gutters, climb up and check for rot behind the gutters, especially if they are sagging. Replace damaged sections of fascia (page 35), removing the gutters where necessary.

# Planning a Roofing Project

Planning makes any project go more smoothly, and working on your roof is no exception.

Measure the square footage of your roof so you can estimate materials and time. When estimating materials, add 15% to allow for waste. Shop around to compare shingle prices, then make a rough cost estimate for the type you select. Count the number of roof elements, like vent pipes, vent fans, skylights, dormers, and chimneys, that you will need to roof around, and tally up the costs for the flashing needed for these elements. Check your sheathing from the attic side. If replacement is needed, make a cost allowance for it. Add in additional materials costs, like building paper, roof cement, nails, dumpster rental, and tool purchase or rental.

Next, estimate the time your project will demand (see chart, next page). Calculate the slope of the roof so you can determine if you need roof jacks to move around. If so, take that into account when making time estimates. By making reasonable estimates, you can divide the project into manageable portions.

Most building centers will deliver shingles, building paper, and other materials directly to your roof, using a mechanical lift. If you can arrange it, have at least one section of the old roof torn off, with new building paper and drip edge installed, before shingle delivery. This will save time, as well as energy you would use to hoist the heavy shingle bundles up from the ground and reposition them on your roof.

**Dress for protection and safety** when working on roof projects. Wear rubber-soled shoes for good traction, knee pads, a nail apron, a tool belt, a long-sleeved shirt, full-length pants, and work gloves. Always wear protective eyewear when nailing or using power tools.

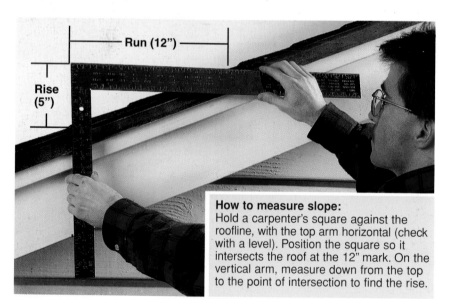

**How to measure slope:**
Hold a carpenter's square against the roofline, with the top arm horizontal (check with a level). Position the square so it intersects the roof at the 12" mark. On the vertical arm, measure down from the top to the point of intersection to find the rise.

**Calculate the slope of your roof** before beginning any roofing project. Slope is usually described by the number of inches the roof rises in each foot along a horizontal plane (called the "run"). For example, the roof shown above has a 5-in-12 slope: it rises 5" in 12" of run. Knowing the slope is important for selecting materials, and to help gauge the difficulty of moving on the roof. Use roof jacks if the slope is 7-in-12 or steeper. Roofs with a slope of 3-in-12 or less must have a fully bonded covering.

## Tips for Planning a Roofing Project

| Estimating time requirements | | | |
|---|---|---|---|
| Task | Time Requirement | Amount | Total Time |
| **Tear-off** | 1 hr./square* | | • |
| **Install building paper** | 30 min./square | | • |
| **Apply shingles:** | | | |
| Flat run | 2 hrs./square | | • |
| Ridges, hips | 30 min./10 ft | | • |
| Dormers** | add 1 hr. ea. | | • |
| **•Flashing:** | | | |
| Chimneys | 2 hrs. ea. | | • |
| Vent pipes | 30 min. ea. | | • |
| Valleys | 30 min./10 ft. | | • |
| Roof vents | 30 min. ea. | | • |
| Skylights | 2 hrs. ea. | | • |
| Drip edge | 30 min./20 ft. | | • |
| **TOTAL TIME FOR PROJECT** | | | • |

NOTE: All time estimates are based on one worker. Reduce time by 40% if there is a helper.

*One square=100 square feet

**Include area of dormer surface in "flat run" estimate

**Protect against damage** from falling materials when tearing off old shingles. Hang tarps over the sides of the house, and lean plywood against the house to protect vegetation.

## How to Install Roof Jacks

"Dead area"

Tip of pry bar over nail heads

**1** Nail roof jacks to the roof at the fourth or fifth course. Position the jacks so the nail slots are in the "dead area" where shingles will not be exposed, then drive a 16d nail into each slot. Install one jack every 4 ft., with 6" to 12" of overhang at the ends of the board.

**2** Shingle over the tops of the roof jacks (when installing shingles), then rest a 2 × 8 or 2 × 10 board on the support arms of the jacks—use the widest board the supports will hold. Drive a nail through the hole in the lip of each roof jack to secure the board.

**3** Remove boards and roof jacks when the project is complete. Drive in 16d nails by positioning the end of a pry bar over each nail head, then rapping the shank of the pry bar with a hammer.

**Choose a roof covering** that is a good match for your house and your budget. *Asphalt or fiberglass shingles* (left) are by far the most popular choice because they are relatively inexpensive, durable, easy to install, and available in a wide variety of styles and colors. Look for shingles with a 20-year warranty. *Wood shakes* (center) are usually made from natural split cedar. They are more expensive and more time-consuming to install than shingles. *Clay tiles* (right) create a very distinctive appearance, but they are fairly expensive and should only be installed by a professional.

# Roofing Materials & Tools

Most do-it-yourselfers select asphalt or fiberglass shingles because they are inexpensive and simple to install. The most common type are "3-tab" shingles, which contain three 12"-wide tabs, separated by slots. Less common coverings, like cedar shakes and clay tiles, are best installed by a professional, but you can save money by doing the tear-off and preparation work yourself. If your roof has a slope of 3-in-12 (page 12) or less, you need a "fully-bonded" roof covering, usually made of built-up tar or sheets of roll roofing that are bonded to the sheathing with roof cement (also a good job for a professional).

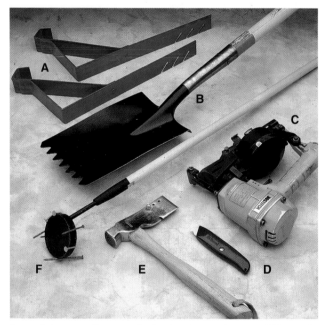

**Specialty roofing tools include:** roof jacks (A), roofing shovel with slots in the blade for tearing off shingles and prying out nails (B), pneumatic nailer (C), utility knife with hook blade (D), roofing hammer with alignment guides and hatchet-style blade (E), and a release magnet for site cleanup (F).

**How to estimate shingles:**
Shingles are sold in bundles, but estimated in *squares*—the amount needed to cover 100 square feet. Three bundles of shingles cover one square. To estimate how many bundles you need, calculate the square footage of roof area, and add 15% for waste. Divide the total by 100, then multiply by 3 to find the number of bundles needed for your project.

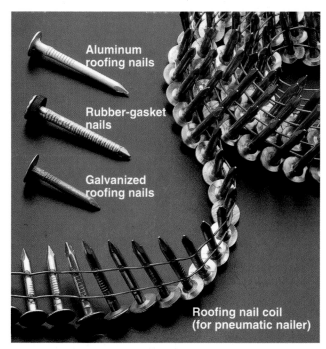

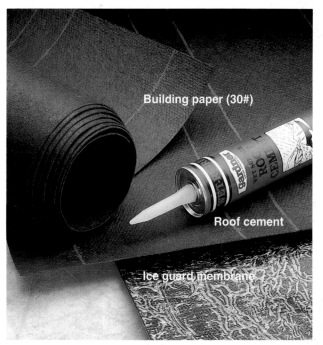

**Use the right fastener for the job.** Use galvanized roofing nails to hand-nail shingles (buy two pounds of nails per square of shingles); use aluminum nails for aluminum flashing, and rubber-gasket nails for galvanized metal flashing. Use roofing nail coils for pneumatic nailers (check coverage chart on carton).

**Common roofing materials include:** 30# building paper for shingle underlayment; cartridges of plastic roofing cement; and ice-guard membrane for use as underlayment in the first course or two of roofs in cold climates (page 18).

**Roof flashing** can be hand-cut or purchased in preformed shapes and sizes. Cut rolled flashing material with aviator snips to make longer flashing pieces, like valley flashing (also available pre-formed), or nonstandard pieces, like base flashing and top saddles (pages 20 to 23). Most experienced roofers buy step flashing blanks in standard sizes, and bend them to fit their project. Drip edge and vent pipe flashing should be purchased as pre-formed pieces. Skylights usually are sold complete with a flashing kit. Complicated flashing pieces, like chimney crickets (page 23), should be made by a professional metalworker.

Cover unshingled sections overnight, using tarps weighted down with shingle bundles. Tear off only one roof section at a time if you cannot reshingle the entire roof in one day.

# Removing Roof Coverings & Replacing Sheathing

Completely remove old shingles, building paper, and flashing if your old roof already has more than one layer of shingles; if shingles are cupped or buckled; or if sheathing is damaged. Replace damaged sheathing after the roof covering is off.

Rent a dumpster from a waste disposal company or your local waste management department, and position it below the roof edge for direct dumping of materials. Or, arrange wheelbarrows on tarps to catch debris. Use extreme caution during tear-off: debris on the roof is a serious hazard.

## Everything You Need:

Tools: dumpster, hammer, chisel, pry bar, roofing knife, roofing shovel, broom, release magnet, rake, tin snips, reciprocating saw, drill.

Materials: protective gear, tarps, plywood sheets, 2 × 4 nailing strips, sheathing material, galvanized deck screws.

## How to Tear Off Old Roof Coverings

**1** Slice through roofing cement around flashing to release it from the shingles. Remove any flashing that you plan to replace. NOTE: Unless the flashing is in exceptional condition, it is easier to remove and replace all the flashing during a full shingle tear-off. Save complicated ʼhing pieces, like chimney saddles or cricke    ʼ reuse, if practical.

**2** Remove the ridge cap, using a pry bar. With the ridge cap out of the way, start prying up the top course of shingles with a roofing shovel or flat pry bar. Work on only one roof section at a time.

**3** Remove old shingles and building paper in large sections, using a roofing shovel. Work from top to bottom. NOTE: The tear-off portion of a roofing project is an ideal time to get help. Having another person to dispose of the materials before they can accumulate on the ground is a great time-saver. Make sure your helper is out of the way before you dump materials.

**4** After removing shingles and building paper from the entire tear-off section, pry out any remaining nails. Also sweep the roof with a garage broom to prepare it for the building paper. TIP: Clean up nails on the ground with a release magnet (page 14).

## How to Replace Damaged Sheathing

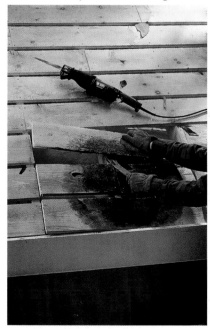

**1** Cut out damaged sheathing boards with a reciprocating saw (check inside for wiring first). Cut next to rafters in an area that extends well beyond the damaged material. Pry out the damaged sections.

**2** Attach 2 x 4 nailing strips at the edges of the cutout sections, flush with the tops of the rafters. Use 3" galvanized deck screws.

**3** Cut sheathing patches from exterior-grade plywood the same thickness as the old sheathing, allowing for a ⅛"-wide expansion gap on all sides. Attach the patch with 2" ck screws or 8d ring-shank s    nails, driven into rafters a       strips.

# Installing Drip Edge & Building Paper

Drip edge is flashing that is installed at the edges of your roof to direct water flow away from the roof sheathing. Building paper is installed on roof decks as insurance in case leaks develop in shingles or flashing. It is sold in several weights, but 30# paper is a good choice for use under shingles (15# meets code in some areas). Check with your local building inspector.

In colder climates, recent changes to building codes require a special type of underlayment, called "ice guard" or "ice shield," instead of standard building paper for the first course or two of underlayment. An adhesive membrane, the ice guard bonds with the sheathing to create a barrier to runoff from ice dams (page 10).

**Work your way up the roof deck** with building paper courses, allowing 4" horizontal overlaps and 12" vertical seams. Roll building paper across valleys from both sides (photo, above), overlapping the ends by 36". Overlap hips and ridges by 6". Attach building paper with a hammer stapler, driving a staple every 6" to 12" at the edges, and one staple per square foot in the field area.

**Everything You Need:**

Tools: hammer, pry bar, roofing knife, hammer stapler, chalk line, tape measure, tin snips.

Materials: drip edge, 30# building paper, roofing cement, ice guard, roofing nails.

## Tips for Installing Drip Edge

Eave edge

Rake edge

**Attach at eaves *before* attaching building paper.** Nail a strip of drip edge along the edge of the eaves. Overlap strips by 2" at vertical seams. Miter the ends at a 45° angle to make a miter joint with the drip edge on the rake edge. Install galvanized and vinyl drip edge with galvanized roofing nails. Use aluminum nails for aluminum drip edge. Nail at 12" intervals.

**Attach at rake edges *after* attaching building paper.** Start at the bottom, forming a miter joint with the drip edge at the eaves. Work toward the ridge, overlapping pieces of drip edge by 2" (make sure the higher strip is on top at overlaps).

# Tips for Installing Building Paper & Ice Guard Underlayment

**Snap a chalk line** 35⅝" up from the eave edge, so the first course of the 36"-wide ice guard membrane (or building paper) overhangs the eaves by ⅜". Install a course of ice guard, using the chalk line as a reference. Peel back the protective backing as you unroll the ice guard. In cold climates, apply as many courses of ice guard as it takes to cover 24" past the roof overhang. In warm climates, ice guard may not be necessary, so check your local codes.

**Measure up from the eave edge** to a point 32" above the top of the previous course of underlayment, and snap another chalk line. Roll out the next course of building paper (or ice guard, if required), overlapping the first course by 4". Install building paper up to the ridge, ruled side up, snapping horizontal lines every two or three rows to check alignment. Always overlap from above. Trim off courses flush with the rake edge.

**Fit a building paper patch** over any obstructions, like vent pipes or roof vents. Apply building paper up to the obstruction, then resume laying the course on the opposite side (make sure to maintain the line). Cut a patch that overlaps the building paper by 12" on all sides. Make a cross-hatch cutout for the obstruction. Position the patch, staple in place, then caulk seams with roof cement.

**Tuck building paper under siding** at the bottoms of dormers and sidewalls, where they intersect with the roof. Also tuck it under counterflashing on chimneys (page 23) and skylights. Carefully pry up the siding, and tuck at least 2" of paper under the siding. Do not refasten siding or counterflashing right away—wait until after you install step flashing (page 22).

# Installing Flashing

Flashing is a metal or rubber barrier used to protect the seams around roof elements. Many beginning roofers consider flashing installation to be the most difficult element of a roofing project. But once you learn one or two basic principles of installing flashing, the mystery disappears quickly.

The purpose of flashing is to make water flow over shingled surfaces, and away from gaps around roof elements, like vent pipes and chimneys. To accomplish this, pieces of flashing are layered between rows of shingles.

Around roof elements, flashing should be secured to one surface only—usually the roof deck. Use only roof cement to bond the flashing to the roof elements. Flashing must be able to flex as the roof element and the roof deck expand and contract (usually at different rates). If flashing is fastened to both the roof deck and the roof element, it will tear or loosen.

NOTE: In this section, we show you how to install flashing during a shingle-installation project (pages 24 to 28). For information on repairing or replacing flashing, see pages 30 to 33. Also see page 15 for flashing product information.

**Bend your own flashing** (top). Make a bending jig by driving screws into a piece of scrap wood, creating a line one-half the width of the flashing when measured from the edge of the board. Clamp the bending jig to a worksurface, then press a step flashing blank (page 15) flat on the board. Bend it over the edge. **Use old flashing as a template** (bottom) for making replacement flashing. This is especially useful for reproducing complicated flashing, like saddle flashing for chimneys or dormers.

## Tip for Installing Flashing

**Replace flashing during shingle installation.** Because most roof flashing is interwoven with shingles, you will get better results than if you try to retrofit flashing around existing shingles.

# How to Install Metal Valley Flashing

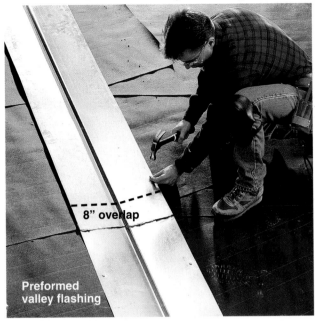

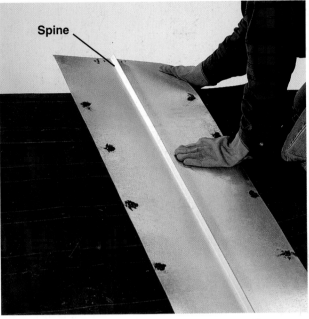

**1** After installing building paper across the valley (page 18), set a piece of valley flashing (preformed or bent from rolled flashing) into the valley, so the bottom of the "V" rests in the crease of the valley. Starting at the eave, nail the flashing near each edge at 12" intervals. Trim the end of the flashing at the eave so it is flush with the drip edges at each side. Add pieces, moving up toward the ridge. Overlap from above by at least 8".

**2** Add overlapping pieces, working toward the ridge, until the flashing reaches a few inches past the ridge. Bend the flashing over the ridge, so it lies flat on the opposite side of the roof. If you are installing pre-formed flashing, make a small cut in the spine for easier bending. Cover nail heads with roof cement (unless you used rubber-gasket nails). Also apply roof cement at the side edges of the flashing.

# How to Install Vent Pipe Flashing

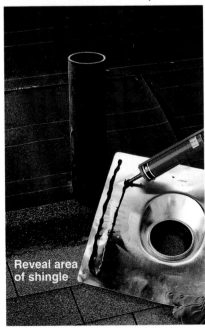

**1** Shingle up to the vent pipe. Cut the top shingle to fit around the pipe, so the "reveal area" of the shingle (the exposed portion) is within 5" of the pipe. Apply roof cement to the base of the flashing.

**2** Slip the sleeve of the flashing over the vent pipe, making sure the pitch of the flange is sloped in the right direction. Press the flange against the roof deck, then fasten with rubber-gasket nails.

**3** Continue installing shingle courses, making cutouts for the pipe. Do not nail through the flash-ing—attach shingles with roof cement where they cover flashing.

## How to Install Step Flashing

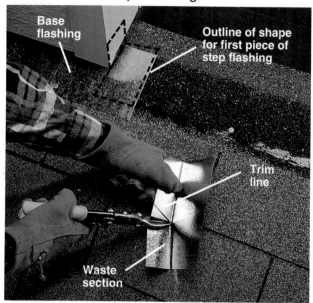

**1** Shingle up to the element requiring flashing (here, a dormer) so the tops of the reveal areas are within 5" of the element. Install base flashing (step 1, next page). Bend a piece of step flashing in half, and set the piece next to the lowest corner of the element. Mark a trim line on the flashing, following the vertical edge of the element. Cut off the waste part of the flashing (the area ouside the trim line on the vertical side of the bend), making a starter cut first.

**2** Pry out the lower courses of siding and any trim at the base of the element. Insert spacers to prop trim or siding away from the work area. Apply roof cement to the base flashing in the area where the overlap with the step flashing will be formed. Tuck the trimmed piece of step flashing under the propped area, and press the flashing into the roof cement. Fasten the flashing with one rubber-gasket nail driven near the top, and into the roof deck.

**3** Apply roof cement to the top side of the first piece of step flashing, where it will be covered by the next shingle course. Install the shingle, setting it firmly into the roof cement. Do not nail through the flashing when attaching shingles. Apply roof cement to the shingle, next to the do____ or other roof element (in the area that will ____ __ by the ne__ piece of step flashing).

**4** Tuck another piece of step flashing under the trim or siding, setting it into the roof cement on the shingle. Overlap the first piece of step flashing by at least 2". Continue flashing in this manner until you reach the top of the element. Trim the last piece of flashing to fit at the top corner of the element. Refasten siding and trim. On chimneys or other elements needing a top saddle (step 3, next page), the saddle should overlap the last piece of step flashing.

# How to Install Chimney Flashing

**1** Shingle up to the chimney base. Cut base flashing, using the old base flashing as a template (page 20). Bend up counterflashing (the flashing anchored in the chimney to cover the step flashing). Apply roof cement to the base of the chimney and the shingles just below the base. Press the base flashing into the roof cement, and bend the flashing around the edges of the chimney. Drive rubber-gasket nails through the flashing flange and into the roof deck.

**2** Apply step flashing and shingles (previous page), working up toward the top of the chimney. Fasten the flashing to the chimney with roof cement only, and fold down counterflashing as you go.

**3** Cut and install top flashing (sometimes called a saddle) around the high side of the chimney, overlapping the final piece of step flashing along each side. Attach with roof cement on both the roof deck and the chimney, and rubber-gasket nails driven through the base of the flashing and into the roof deck. Continue shingling past the chimney, using roof cement (not nails) to attach shingles over flashing.

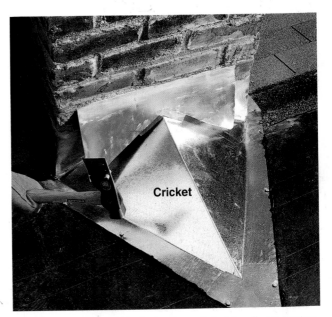

**TIP:** If your roof originally had a cricket to divert water around the chimney, have a new cricket made by a metalworker. Provide the fabricator with either the old cricket to use as a template, or the roof slope (page 12) and the chimney width to use as a guide. Secure the cricket in place with roof cement on all flanges, and drive rubber-gasket nails through the base flanges and into the roof deck. Bend counterflashing back down and fill the gaps with cement.

**Stagger shingles** for effective protection against leaks. If the tab slots are aligned in successive rows, water forms channels, increasing erosion of the mineral surface of the shingles. Creating a 6" offset between rows of shingles (with the 3-tab shingles shown above) ensures that the tab slots do not align.

# Shingling a Roof

If you have the time and the energy, shingling a roof can be a straightforward project that is well within the abilities of most do-it-yourselfers. The most common type of shingles, asphalt 3-tabs, are self-sealing and self-aligning. Installation is mainly a matter of persistence and making sure you follow your lines and shingle pattern.

Because most roof flashing is interwoven into the shingle pattern, be prepared to install all your flashing (pages 20 to 23) during the shingling process. Install building paper and drip edge before you start (pages 18 to 19).

**Everything You Need:**

Tools: tape measure, roofing hammer, pneumatic nailer (optional), pry bar, roofing knife, chalk line, carpenter's square, straightedge, roof jacks and 2 × 10 lumber, aviator snips.

Materials: roofing nails, nailing cartridges (optional), roof cement, flashing, shingles.

## How to Shingle a Roof with 3-tab Shingles

**1** Snap a chalk line onto the first course of ice guard or building paper, 11½" up from the eave edge, to create an alignment line for the starter course of shingles. This will result in a ½" shingle overhang past the edge of the roof for standard 12" shingles. TIP: Do not use red chalk—it will stain roofing materials.

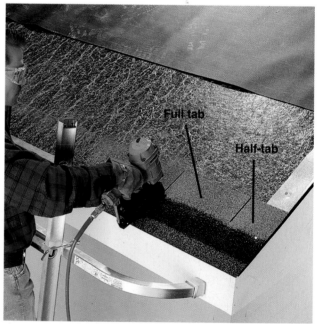

Full tab

Half-tab

**2** Install the starter row: Trim off one-half (6") of an end tab on one shingle. Position the shingle so the tabs are aligned with the chalk line, with the half-tab flush against the rake edge. Drive ⅞" roofing nails near each end, and about 1" down from each slot between tabs. Butt a full shingle next to the trimmed shingle, and nail in place. Fill out the row, trimming the last shingle flush with the opposite rake edge.

**3** Apply the first full course of shingles over the starter course, with the tabs pointing down. Begin at the rake edge where you began the starter row. The first shingle should overhang the rake edge by ⅜", and overhang the eave edge by ½". Make sure the tops of the shingles are flush with the tops of the shingles in the starter course, following the chalk line.

**4** Snap a chalk line from the eave edge to the ridge to create a vertical shingle alignment line. Choose an area with no obstructions, as close as possible to the center of the roof. The chalk line should pass through a slot or a shingle edge on the first full shingle course. Use a carpenter's square to establish a line that is perpendicular with the eave edge.

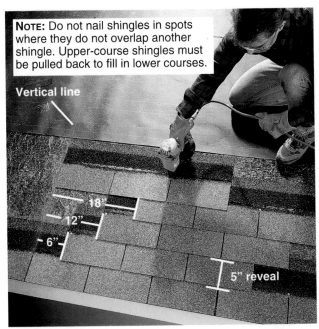

NOTE: Do not nail shingles in spots where they do not overlap another shingle. Upper-course shingles must be pulled back to fill in lower courses.

Vertical line

18"
12"
6"
5" reveal

**5** Use the vertical line to establish a shingle pattern with slots that are offset by 6" in succeeding courses. Tack down a shingle 6" to one side of the vertical line to start the second course. The bottom of the shingle should be 5" above the bottoms of the first-course shingles. Tack down shingles for the third and fourth courses 12" and 18" away from the vertical line. Start the fifth course against the vertical line.

**6** Fill in shingles in the second through fifth courses, working upward from the second course and maintaining a consistent 5" reveal. Slide lower-course shingles under any upper-course shingles left partially nailed, then nail down. NOTE: Install roof jacks, if needed, after filling out the fifth course (page 13).

(continued next page)

# How to Shingle a Roof with 3-tab Shingles (continued)

**TIP:** Check the alignment of your shingles after each four-course cycle. In several spots on the top course, measure from the bottom edges of the shingles to the nearest building-paper line. If you discover any misalignment, distribute adjustments over the next few rows until the misalignment is corrected.

**7** When you reach obstructions, like dormers, shingle a full course above them so you can retain your shingle offset pattern. On the unshingled side of the obstruction, snap another vertical reference line, using the shingles above the obstruction as a guide.

**8** Shingle upward from the ___ve ___ the other side of the obstruction, using the ___ line ___ a reference for reestablishing your ___ pattern. Fill out the shingle ___ou___ ___ ___e edges of the roof, then trir off t___ 15).

**9** Trim off some of the excess shingle material at the the "V"s in valley flashing wherever two roof decks join (these edges will be trimmed back farther at a slight taper after both roof decks are shingled). Do not cut into flashing.

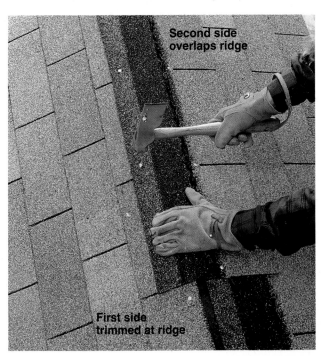

**10** Install shingles on adjoining roof decks, starting at the bottom edge, using the same offset alignment pattern used on the other roof decks (steps 1 to 6). Install shingles until courses overlap the center of the valley flashing at the joint between roof decks. Trim shingles at both sides of the valley when finished (step 14).

**11** When you reach a hip (any peak where two sections of roof meet) or the ridge (the hip at the top of your roof), shingle up the first roof side until the tops of the uppermost reveal areas are within 5" of the hip or ridge. Trim the excess off along the joint at the peak. Overlap the ridge or hip (no more than 5") with the top shingle course on the other side of the peak.

TIP: Cut three 12"-square ridge/hip caps from each 3-tab shingle. With the top surface facing down, cut the shingles at the tab lines, trimming off both top corners of the 12"-square cap shingles (trimming corners prevents unsightly overlaps in the reveal area).

**12** Snap a chalk line 6" down from the hip or ridge on one side, parallel to the peak. Begin attaching cap shingles at one end, aligned with the chalk line. Drive two roofing nails per cap, about 1" in from each edge, just below the seal strip.

(continued next page)

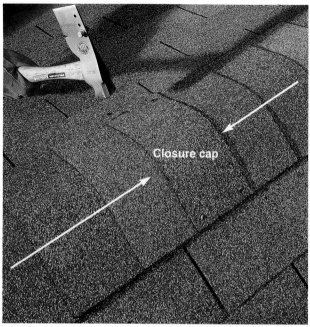

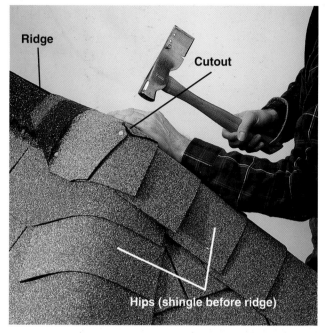

**13** Install cap shingles halfway along the ridge or hip, creating a 5" reveal for each cap. Follow the chalk line. Then, starting at the opposite end of the ridge or hip, install caps over the other half of the roof. Cut a 5"-wide section from the reveal area of a shingle tab, and use it as a "closure cap" to cover the joint where the caps meet.

**VARIATION:** Wherever roof hips join with roof ridges, shingle to the top of each hip with cap shingles. Then, make a cutout in the center of a ridge cap, set the cap at the end of the ridge, and bend the corners so they fit over the hips. Secure each corner with a roofing nail, and cover nail heads with roof cement.

**14** After all shingles are installed, trim the shingles at the valleys to create a gap that is 3" wide at the ridge, and widens at a rate of per foot toward the eave edge. Use a utility knife a roofing blade and a straightedge (b are cut through the valley flashing underesides and edges o Also cover any e ent.

**15** Trim the shingles at the rake edges of the roof, using a utility knife with a hooked roofing blade (or you can use aviator snips). Leave a ⅜" overhang. Always use a straightedge to ensure a straight cut.

## Variation: How to Shingle Over an Old Roof

Trim new shingles to fit

**1** Cut tabs off shingles and install the remaining strips over the reveal area of the old first course, creating a flat surface for the starter row of new shingles. Use 1¼"-long roofing nails. NOTE: Read the section on shingling a roof (pages 24 to 28) before you start.

**2** Trim the tops off shingles for the first course. The shingles should be sized to butt against the bottom edges of the old third course, overhanging the roof edge by ½". Install the shingles so the tab slots do not align with the slots in the old shingles.

Cutout in old shingles to create a flat surface for the base flange of vent pipe flashing

**3** Using the old shingles to direct your layout, begin installing the new shingles. Maintain a consistent tab slot offset (page 25, step 5). Shingle up toward the roof ridge, stopping before the final course. Install flashing as you proceed (see next step). If valley flashing is in good condition, it does not need to be replaced.

**4** Replace old flashing during the shingling sequence (pages 20 to 23). A "roofover" is flashed using the same techniques and materials used for shingling over building paper, except you need to trim or fill in shingles around vent pipes and roof vents to create a flat face for the base flange of the flashing pieces.

**5** Tear off old hip and ridge caps before shingling the hips and ridges. Replace old hip and ridge caps after all other shingling is completed (pages 27 to 28).

# Repairing Shingles & Flashing

Roof materials that have sustained minimal damage or wear can be patched or repaired, avoiding the expense and work of replacing some or all of your roof. Plastic roof cement and rolled, galvanized flashing can be used for many simple roof repairs. TIP: Heat brittle shingles with a hair dryer to make them easier to handle.

## Everything You Need:

Tools: hammer, pry bar, caulk gun, utility knife with roofing blade, pointed trowel, hacksaw, rubber mallet.

Materials: flashing, roof coverings, roof cement, roofing nails, 30# building paper.

**Use plastic roof cement for a variety of minor repairs,** like reattaching loose shingles. Wipe down the building paper and the underside of the shingle, let them dry, then apply roof cement liberally. Seat the shingle in the bed of cement.

## Tips for Making Repairs with Roof Cement

**Tack down buckled shingles** _____ out below the buckled area, filling with _____ and pressing the shingle in the cer____ _____ of cement to patch cracks__ oth__ _____ blems. See page 10 for mo__ _____ shin____.

**Seal gaps around flashing** by cleaning out the old roof cement and replacing it with fresh roof cement. Joints around flashing are common places for roof leaks to occur.

# How to Replace a Section of Shingles

**1** Pull out damaged shingles in the repair area, beginning with the uppermost shingle. Be careful not to damage any surrounding shingles that are in good condition.

**2** Remove old nails with a flat pry bar. Exposed nail heads will cause punctures in new shingles. Important: remove nails in the shingle above the repair area to enable you to nail new shingles. Cover holes or damage in the building paper with roof cement.

**3** Install replacement shingles, beginning with the lowest shingle in the repair area. Nail above tab slots with ⅞" or 1" roofing nails. TIP: Asphalt shingles can be aged to match surrounding shingles by wiping the surface with mineral spirits. Rinse before installing.

Seal line

**4** Install all but the top shingle with nails (pages 24 to 25), then apply roof cement to the underside of the top shingle, above the seal line.

**5** Slip last s... ...ce under the overlapping shingle. P... ...into the roof cement. Lift up the shi... ...re air a..., and nail the top r...acem...

## How to Replace Wood Shakes & Shingles

**1** Split the damaged shake (shown) or shingle, using a ⸏ammer and chisel, and remove ⸏ pieces. Pry out (cut nails in ⸏rlapping shingles with a hack- ⸏ blade slipped underneath the ⸏gle).

**2** Gently pry up shingles or shakes above the repair area. Cut new shingles or shakes for the lowest course, leaving about ⅜" for expansion. Nail replacement pieces in place with ring-shank siding nails. Fill in all but the top course.

**3** Cut pieces for the top course, slip them beneath the overlapping shingles, and face-nail them in place near the tops. Cover all exposed nail heads with roof cement, then wipe off the excess. TIP: Apply wood sealer or stain to "weather" new material.

## ⸏w to Patch Damaged Flashing

**1** Measure the damaged area and cut a patch from flashing material of the same type as the original flashing. The patch should be wide enough to slip under the shingles at each side of the repair area. Break the seal between the valley flashing and the shingles around the damaged area. Scrub the damaged flashing with a wire brush, and wipe clean.

**2** Apply a bed of roof cement to the back side of the patch, then slip the patch under the shingles on each side of the repair area. Press the patch securely into the roof cement. Add cement at the seams and the shingle joints. Feather out the cement to prevent damming of water. NOTE: New flashing material will blend in quickly as natural forces cause the metal to discolor.

# How to Replace Step Flashing

**1** Carefully bend up counterflashing (or pry out siding) covering the damaged step flashing. Cut roof cement seals, and pull back the shingles covering damaged step flashing. Remove the damaged piece or pieces of flashing with a flat pry bar.

**2** Cut new step flashing from the same type of metal (aluminum or galvanized steel) used for the old flashing. Apply roof cement to the flashing on both unexposed sides. Slip the flashing into place, making sure it is overlapped by the flashing above it, and that it overlaps the flashing below. It also must overlap the shingle beneath it. Drive one roofing nail through the flashing at the bottom corner, and into the roof deck. Do not fasten to the roof element.

**3** Bend counterflashing back down, and seal the counterflashing seams with roof cement.

**4** Lift shingles next to the repair area, then apply fresh roof cement to the undersides and to any exposed nail heads. Press the shingles down against the flashing to create a bond. Do not nail flashing when attaching shingles.

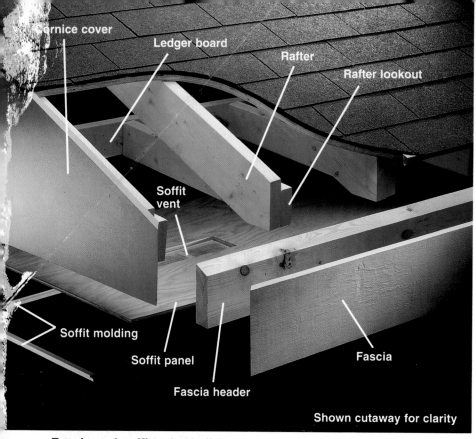

Cornice cover
Ledger board
Rafter
Rafter lookout
Soffit vent
Soffit molding
Soffit panel
Fascia header
Fascia

Shown cutaway for clarity

**Fascia and soffits** close off the eave area beneath the roof overhang. The fascia covers the ends of rafters and rafter lookouts, and provides a surface for attaching gutters. Soffits are protective panels that span the area between the fascia and the side of the house. Some soffit types attach to fascia headers (above), while others fit into grooves cut in the back sides of the fascia. Soffit moldings and ledger boards are used to mount the soffit panels at the side of the house.

## Option: Install a New Soffit System

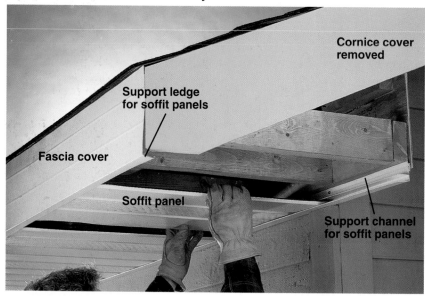

Cornice cover removed
Support ledge for soffit panels
Fascia cover
Soffit panel
Support channel for soffit panels

**Install a new soffit system** if your old system has failed, or pests have infested the open eave areas of your roof overhang. A complete soffit system consists of fabricated fascia covers, soffit panels (nonventilated or ventilated), and support channels that hold the panels at the sides of your house. Most soffit systems sold at building centers are made of aluminum or vinyl. Follow manufacturer's instructions for installation.

# Repairing Fascia & Soffits

Fascia and soffits add a finished look to your roof, and promote a healthy roof system. A well-ventilated fascia/soffit system prevents moisture from building up under the roof and in the attic. A secure system keeps pests, like birds and bats, from nesting in the eaves.

Usually fashioned from dimension lumber, fascia is attached to rafters or rafter lookouts (photo, left). While enhancing the appearance of your home, it also provides a stable surface for hanging gutters.

Repairing fascia and soffits is easy. Most problems can be corrected by cutting out the damaged material and replacing it with new material. Joints between fascia boards are lock-nailed (page 35), so you should remove whole sections of fascia to make accurate miter cuts for patches. Soffits usually are not removed for repairs (pages 36 to 37).

Fasten soffit and fascia material with ring-shank siding nails, or use galvanized deck screws. Nails are easier to work with in some cases, but screws provide more holding power.

Whenever repairing soffits, take a moment to inspect vents in the system for sufficient air flow (pages 44 to 46).

## Everything You Need:

Tools: circular saw, jig saw, drill, hammer, flat pry bar, chisel, nail set.

Materials: replacement materials to match damaged parts, nailing strips, nails or screws, caulk, primer, paint.

# How to Repair Fascia

**1** Remove gutters, shingle moldings, and any other material that prevents removal of the damaged section of fascia.

**Shingle molding**

**2** Using a flat pry bar, remove the entire damaged section all the way to the next fascia board. Remove old nails.

**3** Cut off the damaged portion of the fascia board. Set your circular saw to make a miter cut, and saw at a rafter location (look for nail holes to identify the rafter location).

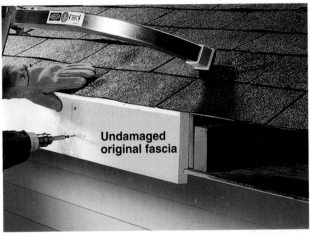

**Undamaged original fascia**

**4** Attach the undamaged original fascia, using 2" galvanized deck screws driven into rafter lookouts or rafters. Cut a patch board with a matching miter at the mating end to replace the damaged section.

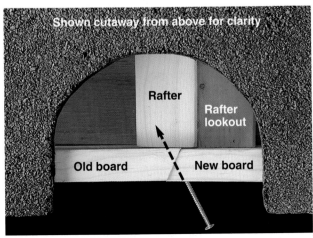

Shown cutaway from above for clarity

**Rafter**

**Rafter lookout**

**Old board** **New board**

**5** Attach the patch board. Drill pilot holes, then drive nails at an angle through the mitered ends of both boards, creating a lock-nail joint.

**6** Reattach the shingle moldings and trim, using 4d galvanized finish nails. Set nail heads. Prime and paint the patch to match the fascia. Reattach gutters.

# How to Repair Wood-panel Soffits

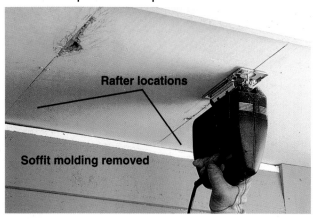

**1** Remove the support molding in the damaged area. Drill entry holes for a jig saw blade, then cut out the soffit area that contains the damage. Saw as close as possible to the rafter or lookout locations. If necessary, finish the cut with a wood chisel.

**2** Remove the damaged soffit section, using a flat pry bar if necessary. Cut nailing strips and attach them to the rafters or rafter lookouts at the edges of the opening (step 2, next page).

**3** Measure the opening, and cut a soffit patch to fit from material similar to the original soffit. Allow ⅛" on all sides for expansion gaps. Make cutouts for existing soffit vents, or for new soffit vents (page 46).

**4** Install the soffit patch by driving 1¼" galvanized deck screws into the nailing strips or rafter lookouts. NOTE: If you do not plan to paint the entire soffit, you may find it easier to prime and paint the patch before installing.

**5** Reattach the soffit molding, using 4d galvanized casing nails.

**6** Fill nail holes, screw holes, and gaps with siliconized acrylic caulk. Smooth out the caulk so it is even with the surface. Prime and paint to match. Install vent covers if needed.

# How to Repair Tongue-and-groove Soffits

**1** Remove the soffit molding. Locate the closest rafter lookout on each side of the damaged area. Drill an entry hole for a jig saw, then cut out the damaged section, cutting as close as possible to the lookout. Pry the damaged section loose. NOTE: To remove width-run tongue-and-groove soffits (inset), cut across the ends of boards near the fascia.

**2** Cut a nailing strip from 2 × 2 stock, and fasten it to the rafter lookout at each end of the opening, using 2½" galvanized deck screws.

**3** Cut patch boards to fit, using similar tongue-and-groove stock. Fasten all but the final board by driving 8d galvanized casing nails through pilot holes in the tongues of the boards, and into the nailing strips. Set the nail heads so the next patch board will fit cleanly over the tongue of the first board.

**Top lip removed**

**4** Trim the top lip from grooved edge of the final board in the installation sequence. Position the board in the opening. Face-nail ring-shank siding nails through the last patch board and into the nailing strips. Prime and paint to match. Attach soffit vents covers, if needed.

**Rehanging sagging gutters** is a common gutter repair. Before rehanging, snap a chalk line that follows the original slope (usually about ¼" per 10 ft. toward the downspouts). To rehang gutters, remove the hangers in and near the sag, and lift the gutter until it is flush with the chalk line. Reattach the hangers (replace them if they are in bad condition), shifting their location slightly so you do not use the original holes. If the hangers are more than 24" apart, or there is no hanger within 12" of a seam, add hangers.

# Repairing Gutters

Gutters channel water away from your home. Clogged, sagging, or leaky gutters can cause extensive damage to your siding, foundation, or landscaping. They can also result in water buildup in your basement.

Evaluate the type and extent of gutter damage to select the appropriate repair method. Often, small leaks and minor damage can be repaired with easy-to-use gutter repair products (next page). Moderate damage to metal gutters can be patched with flashing (pages 40 to 41). TIP: Prevent corrosion by patching with the same type of metal (usually aluminum or galvanized steel) from which the gutters are made.

If the damaged area is more than 2 ft. in length, replace the entire section of gutter with new material (page 41). To locate a section of gutter for making repairs, trace the profile of your existing gutters and take it with you to the building center. Also measure the gutter at the widest point—if your gutters are more than 15 years old, they likely are a little larger than gutters made today. Check salvage yards, or have a new section custom-bent by a metal fabricator.

If your gutters are beyond repair, remove and replace them. Snap-together vinyl gutters (pages 42 to 43) are popular with today's homeowners.

If your house has wood gutters, patch small holes or rot with epoxy wood filler. If damage is more serious, contact a professional carpenter.

## Everything You Need:

Tools: utility knife, stiff-bristled or wire brush, abrasive pads, aviator snips, screwdriver, pry bar, hammer, portable drill, hacksaw, caulk gun.

Materials: gutter caulk, gutter patching kit, roof cement, flashing material, gutter fasteners.

## Gutter Accessories

**Install gutter guards** to prevent buildup of debris in the gutters. Buy guards that match the size and style of your gutters. Common mesh gutter guards (above) usually require mesh supports. **Downspout strainers** at the outlets prevent debris from collecting in downspouts, where clogs are hard to remove.

**Install a swing-up elbow** at the end of each drain pipe, allowing the outlet pipe to be lifted out of the way when you are working near the foundation of the house. Add a **splash block** to prevent erosion and help direct runoff away from your house.

## Tips for Using Gutter Repair Products

**Use gutter caulk** to fill small holes and seal minor leaks. Usually made with a butyl-rubber base, gutter caulk flexes without losing its seal. It is also resistant to the elements.

**Use gutter patching kits** for temporary repairs to gutters with minor damage. Read the manufacturer's recommendations and directions before purchasing and using repair products. For long-term repairs, see pages 40 to 41.

## How to Patch Metal Gutters

**1** Clean the area around the damage with a wire brush. Scrub with an abrasive pad to loosen residue, then clean the area with water.

**2** Apply a ⅛"-thick layer of roof cement evenly over the damage, and spread it a few inches beyond the damaged area on all sides.

**3** Cut and bend a patch from flashing made from the same material as the gutters. Bed the patch in the roof cement, and feather the cement so it will not cause significant damming.

## How to Repair Leaky Joints

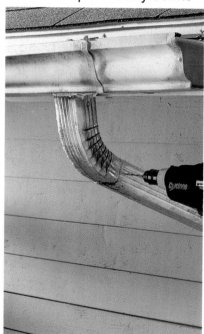

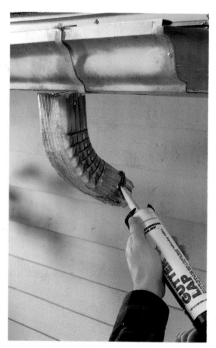

**1** Drill out rivets or remove metal screws that secure the joint. Disassemble the damaged joint. With downspouts, you may need to disassemble the entire downspout to get the bad joint apart.

**2** Scrub both parts of the joint, using a stiff-bristled brush (for vinyl gutters) or a wire brush (for metal gutters). Clean the damaged area with water.

**3** When dry, apply caulk to the joining parts, then reassemble the joint. Reinforce with new fasteners, adding new hangers if the originals need replacing.

# How to Replace a Section of Metal Gutter

**1** Remove gutter hangers in or near the damaged area. TIP: Insert wood spacers in the gutter, near each hanger, before putting pressure on the gutter. This helps protect gutters from damage.

**2** Slip spacers between the gutter and fascia, near each end of the damaged area, so you do not damage the roof when cutting the gutter. Cut out the damaged area with a hacksaw.

**3** Cut a gutter patch from material similar in type, size, and profile to the original gutter. The patch should be at least 4" longer than the damaged section.

**4** With a wire brush, clean the cut ends of the old gutter. Caulk the ends, then center the gutter patch over the damage and press into caulk.

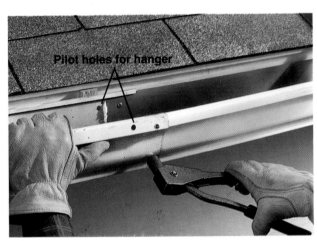

**5** Secure the gutter patch with pop rivets or sheet metal screws. Use at least three or four fasteners at each joint. On the inside surfaces of the gutter, caulk over the heads of the fasteners.

**6** Install the gutter hangers, using new hangers if necessary (do not use old holes). Prime and paint the patch to match.

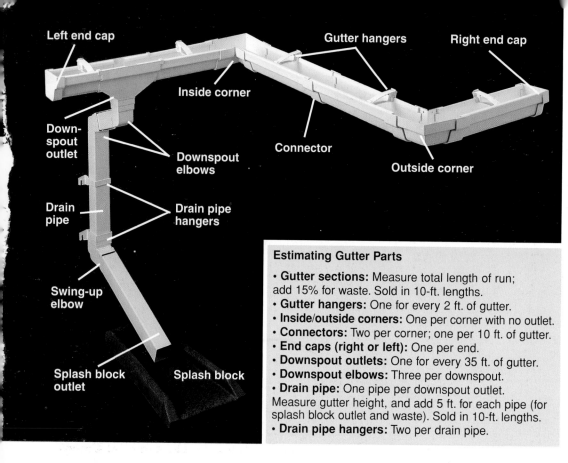

Left end cap
Gutter hangers
Right end cap
Inside corner
Down-spout outlet
Downspout elbows
Connector
Outside corner
Drain pipe
Drain pipe hangers
Swing-up elbow
Splash block outlet
Splash block

**Vinyl snap-together gutter systems** are becoming increasingly popular. Easy to install and relatively inexpensive, they will not rot or deteriorate. The slip joints allow for expansion and contraction. Before you purchase and install new gutters, make a cost estimate. Do not base the estimate solely on the advertised prices of gutter and drain pipe sections, which make up only a fraction of the final cost of the system.

**Estimating Gutter Parts**

- **Gutter sections:** Measure total length of run; add 15% for waste. Sold in 10-ft. lengths.
- **Gutter hangers:** One for every 2 ft. of gutter.
- **Inside/outside corners:** One per corner with no outlet.
- **Connectors:** Two per corner; one per 10 ft. of gutter.
- **End caps (right or left):** One per end.
- **Downspout outlets:** One for every 35 ft. of gutter.
- **Downspout elbows:** Three per downspout.
- **Drain pipe:** One pipe per downspout outlet. Measure gutter height, and add 5 ft. for each pipe (for splash block outlet and waste). Sold in 10-ft. lengths.
- **Drain pipe hangers:** Two per drain pipe.

# Installing a Vinyl Snap-together Gutter System

Installing a new gutter system is a manageable task for most homeowners. Snap-together gutter systems are designed for ease of installation, requiring no fasteners other than the screws used to attach the gutter hangers to the fascia.

Draw a detailed plan before purchasing and installing new gutters. See the chart above for tips on planning and estimating. If you have never installed gutters before, you may find it helpful to test-fit all the pieces on the ground, following your plan, before you begin the actual installation.

**Everything You Need:**

Tools: chalk line, tape measure, drill, hacksaw.

Materials: 1¼" deck screws, gutters and drain pipes, connectors, and fittings (see above).

## How to Install Vinyl Snap-together Gutters

Slope= ¼" per 10 ft.

Fascia

**1** Mark a point at the high end of each gutter run, 1" down from the top of the fascia. Snap chalk lines that slope ¼" per 10 ft. toward downspout outlets. For runs longer than 35 ft., mark a slope from a high point in the center toward downspouts at each end.

**2** Install downspout outlets near the ends of gutter runs (at least one outlet for every 35 ft. of run). The tops of the outlets should be flush with the slope line, and they should align with end caps on the corners of your house, where drain pipes will be attached.

**3** Attach hangers or support clips for hangers (some models) for a complete run, following the manufacturer's directions. Attach to fascia at 24" intervals, using 1¼" deck screws. Follow the slope line.

**4** Attach outside and inside corners at corner locations that do not have downspout outlets or end caps. Follow the slope line.

**5** Cut gutter sections to fit between outlets and corners, using a hacksaw. Attach end cap, and connect gutter section to outlet. Cut gutter sections to fit between outlets, allowing for expansion gaps. Test-fit.

**6** On the ground, join the gutter sections together using connectors. Attach gutter hangers to the gutters (for models with support clips mounted on fascia). Hang the gutters, connecting to the outlets.

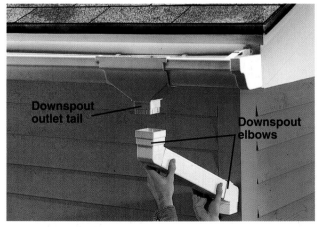

**7** Cut a section of drain pipe to fit between two downspout elbows—one elbow should fit over the tail of the downspout outlet, the other fits against the wall. Assemble the parts, slip the top elbow onto the outlet, and secure the other with a drain pipe hanger.

**8** Cut a piece of drain pipe to fit between the elbow at the top of the wall (step 7) and the end of the drain pipe run (at least 12" above the ground). Attach an elbow to the end of the pipe, and secure to the wall with a drain-pipe hanger. Add accessories (page 39).

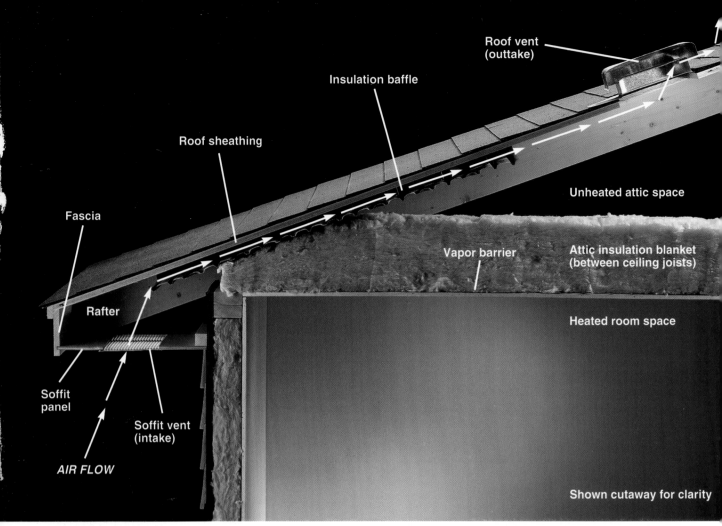

Roof vent
(outtake)

Insulation baffle

Roof sheathing

Fascia

Unheated attic space

Vapor barrier

Attic insulation blanket
(between ceiling joists)

Rafter

Heated room space

Soffit
panel

Soffit vent
(intake)

AIR FLOW

Shown cutaway for clarity

**Sufficient air flow** prevents heat build-up in your attic, and helps protect your roof from damage caused by condensation or ice. A typical ventilation system has vents in the soffits to admit fresh air, which flows upward beneath the roof sheathing and exits through roof vents.

# Installing Soffit & Roof Vents

An effective ventilation system equalizes temperatures on both sides of the roof, which helps keep your house cooler in the summer and prevents ice dams at the roof eaves in cold climates.

The best strategy for increasing roof ventilation is to add more of the existing types of vents. If you are reroofing, however, consider replacing all your roof vents with a continuous ridge vent (next page). You can increase outtake ventilation by replacing a standard roof vent with an electric turbine vent, but an easier solution is simply to add another standard roof vent.

### Everything You Need:

Tools: hammer, caulk gun, drill, jig saw, tape measure, pry bar, pencil, utility knife.
Materials: roofing nails, roof cement, stainless steel screws, soffit vent covers, roof vents.

## Determining Ventilation Requirements

**Measure attic floor space** to determine how much ventilation you need. You should have one square foot each of intake and outtake vents for every 150 square feet of unheated attic floor space.

# Common Intake Ventilation Types

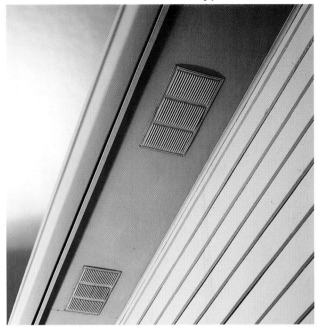

**Soffit vents** can be added to increase air flow into attics on houses with a closed soffit system. Make sure there is an unobstructed air passage from the soffit area to the roof before you install new soffit vents (page 46).

**Continuous soffit vents** provide even air flow into attics. They are usually installed during new construction, but they can be added as retrofits to unvented soffit panels.

# Common Outtake Ventilation Types

**Roof vents** can be added near the ridge line when you need to increase outtake ventilation. Fixed roof vents are easy to install (page 47) and have no mechanical parts that can break down.

**Gable and dormer vents** generally are installed instead of soffit vents—especially on houses with open eaves. Covers come in a variety of styles and colors to match siding.

**Continuous ridge vents** create an even outtake air flow because they span the entire ridge. Barely noticeable from the ground, ridge vents are usually installed during roof construction, but can be added during a reroofing project.

## How to Install a Soffit Vent

**1** Examine the eave area from inside your attic to make sure there is nothing obstructing air flow from the soffits. If insulation is blocking the air passage, install insulation baffles (page 49).

**2** Draw a cutout for the soffit vent cover on the soffit panel. Center the vents between the fascia and the side of the house. The cover outline should be ¼" smaller on all sides than the soffit vent cover.

**3** Drill a starter hole, then cut the vent openings with a jig saw.

**4** Caulk the flanges of the vent cover with siliconized acrylic caulk. Screw the vent cover to the soffit. TIP: For visual effect, install all of the new vent covers with the louvers pointing in the same direction.

## How to Install a Roof Vent

**1** Mark the location for the roof vent by driving a nail through the roof sheathing. The nail should be centered between rafters, and between 16" and 24" from the ridge pole.

**2** Locate the marker nail, and center the vent cover over the nail. Outline the base flange of the vent cover on the shingles, then remove shingles in an area 2" inside the outline. Mark the roof-vent hole using the marker nail as a centerpoint. Cut the hole with a reciprocating saw or jig saw.

**3** Apply roof cement to the underside of the base flange. Set the vent cover in position, slipping the base flange under the shingles, centered over the vent-hole cutout.

**4** Secure the roof vent to the sheathing with rubber gasket nails on all sides of the flange. Tack down any loose shingles. Do not nail through the base flange when attaching shingles.

# Insulating & Weatherizing Products

**(A) A vapor barrier** prevents condensation from occurring around insulation. Use 6-mil poly as a vapor barrier for rigid insulation boards or unfaced fiberglass insulation (page 49).

**(B) Faced fiberglass insulation** has an attached vapor barrier. More expensive than unfaced insulation, it is especially useful in areas, like crawl spaces, where the vapor barrier must be on the opposite side from which the insulation is installed.

**(C) An attic blanket** is a common type of unfaced fiberglass insulation. Unfaced insulation is less costly than faced insulation and, when used with a solid poly vapor barrier, it provides better protection from mois-

ture. Sold in rolls and flat batts sized to fit standard stud cavities.

**(D) Rigid insulation boards** are attached directly to basement walls, usually with panel adhesive. Urethane foam insulation (shown) is sturdy and a good insulator. Inexpensive open-cell foam boards can be used, but they are harder to work with. Rigid boards are sold in thicknesses ranging from ½" to 2".

**(E) Baffles** are attached to the rafters at the sill plate in your attic. Usually made of plastic or polystyrene, they ensure that attic insulation does not obstruct the air flow across the underside of the roof.

# Improving Insulation

Adding insulation to attics or basement walls is a quick and easy do-it-yourself project that has an immediate payback in energy savings.

Most local building codes require minimum amounts of insulation for new construction. Check with your building inspector—these minimum requirements make good guidelines for owners of older homes as well. Guidelines for insulation are given in terms of total "R-value," which measures the ability of materials to resist the flow of heat (see chart below).

In this section we show you how to install a fiberglass attic blanket. For most homeowners this is a simpler and cleaner type of attic insulation than loose, blown insulation. Attics with existing insulation should have a vapor barrier in place: use unfaced insulation. Rigid boards are good for basement walls because they pack greater R-value into smaller spaces, and they can be attached directly to walls with panel adhesive.

**Install baffles** to keep new attic insulation from blocking the flow of air through your attic. You can purchase and install ready-made baffles, or make your own from plywood or rigid insulation board. For more information on ventilation, see pages 44 to 47.

### Everything You Need:

Tools: tape measure, utility knife, straightedge, plumb line, insulation board saw, staple gun.

Materials: 6-mil poly vapor barrier, baffles, insulation, 2 × 2 furring strips, construction adhesive, rigid foam insulation, panel adhesive.

### Recommended insulation amounts

|  | Cold climate | Moderate climate |
|---|---|---|
| Attic: | R38 | R26 |
| Wall: | R19 | R19 |
| Floor: | R22 | R11 |

### Insulation thickness chart:

| Fiberglass | | Open-cell foam: | |
|---|---|---|---|
| R11 (faced) | 3½" | R4 | 1" |
| R13 (unfaced) | 3½" | R6 | 1½" |
| R19 (unfaced) | 6" | R8 | 2" |
| R21 (high density) | 5¼" | **Urethane foam:** | |
| R25 (unfaced) | 8" | R5 | 1" |
| R30 (unfaced) | 10" | R10 | 2" |

**Resistance value (R-value)** measures the ability of a material to resist heat flow. The charts above show minimum R-values for different areas (often obtained by combining two layers). Use the lower chart to determine how much insulation you can install in a specific area (never compress insulation).

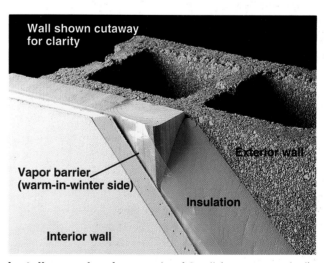

Wall shown cutaway for clarity

Exterior wall

Vapor barrier (warm-in-winter side)

Insulation

Interior wall

**Install vapor barriers** made of 6-mil (recommended) or 4-mil poly on the warm-in-winter side of insulation. Vapor barriers protect the insulation and the structural members of your house from condensation that can occur when warm, humid air meets cold air. When layering insulation, install one vapor barrier only.

# Tips for Insulating Your House

SAFETY TIP: Always wear a long-sleeved shirt, gloves, and a particle mask or respirator when handling fiberglass insulation.

**Install fiberglass insulation** between floor joists over crawl spaces or unheated basements. Make sure the vapor barrier faces up, and install chicken wire or insulation support rods below to hold the insulation in place.

**Insulate the rim joist** at the top of your foundation walls by filling it loosely with fiberglass insulation. Pack the insulation just tightly enough that it does not fall out.

**Insulate garage walls** in attached garages. Use faced fiberglass insulation, with the vapor barrier facing into the garage. Cover with wall covering, like wallboard, especially in areas that are vulnerable to damage.

# Tips for Installing Insulation

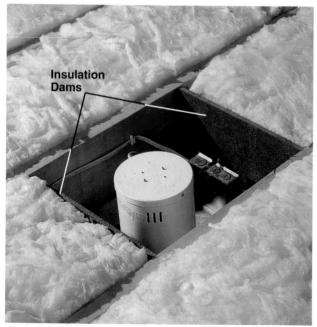

Insulation Dams

**Make insulation dams** from rigid boards and install them between ceiling joists to keep attic insulation at least 6" away from recessed lights, vents fans, and other electrical fixtures that generate heat. Check the fixture to see if it is "IC" rated for insulation contact. If it is IC rated, no dams are needed.

**Do not compress insulation** to fit a spot. Insulation needs air space within the material to be effective in resisting heat transfer. If the insulation you want to install is too thick, trim or tear it to match the depth of the wall, ceiling, or floor cavity.

# How to Insulate Your Attic

**1** Measure the depth of existing insulation, and calculate how much additional insulation, if any, is required (see page 49, chart). TIP: When working over exposed joists, lay a sheet of plywood across the joists to create a stable working surface.

**2** Attach baffles to the roof sheathing or rafters to keep new insulation from blocking the air flow along the roof sheathing. Baffles should extend past the bottoms of the ceiling joists.

**3** Cut rolls of unfaced fiberglass insulation to length in a well-ventilated work area, using a straightedge and a utility knife. For attics with uneven joist spacing, you will need to trim a few pieces for width as well.

**4** Roll out insulation, starting at the farthest point from the attic access. NOTE: Attic blankets may be piled higher than the tops of the joists as long as you do not plan to use your attic for storage.

**OPTION:** For greater insulation (especially in colder climates), roll out a second attic blanket layer perpendicular to the first layer. Do not use faced insulation or another layer of vapor barrier.

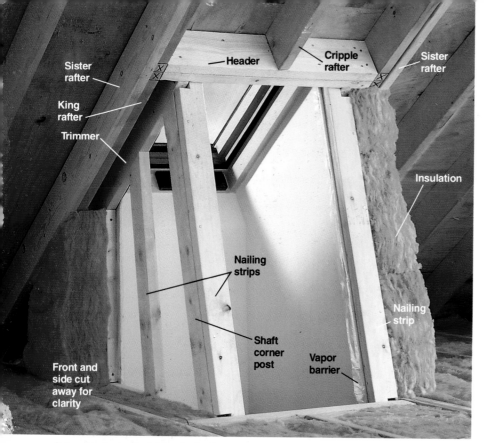

Sister rafter

King rafter

Trimmer

Header

Cripple rafter

Sister rafter

Insulation

Nailing strips

Nailing strip

Shaft corner post

Vapor barrier

Front and side cut away for clarity

**A typical skylight installation** requires a framed opening in the roof to hold the skylight, another opening in the ceiling, and a framed shaft that joins the two openings. In a home with rafter construction, one or two rafters may be cut to make room for a large skylight, as long as the openings are reinforced with double headers and "sister" framing members. The shaft is made with 2 × 4 lumber and wallboard, and includes a vapor barrier and fiberglass insulation.

Nailing flange

Step flashing

**Weatherproof your skylight** with metal flashing on all sides. Even if your window has a "self-flashing" mounting flange, it is a good idea to install additional flashings. Flashing kits, available from skylight manufacturers, include step flashings (shown above), a sill flashing to fit the bottom of the window, and a head flashing to fit the top. Sheet-metal shops can fabricate flashings according to your measurements.

# Installing a Skylight

A skylight (sometimes called a roof window) is an ideal way to provide additional light and ventilation in areas where standard windows are not practical.

Many homeowners have resisted installing skylights because older models were prone to leakage. But today's skylights, with metal-clad frames and pre-attached flashings, are extremely reliable. When installed correctly, good skylights have the same life-expectancy as windows.

If your roof is supported with trusses, choose a narrow skylight that fits between the trusses. Roof trusses should never be cut. If your roof is supported with rafters, you can safely cut and remove one or two rafters to frame the skylight opening.

Many people install skylights in direct sunlight, but in warmer climates, it is better to install them on the north side of the roof or in shaded areas.

This section includes:

- Installing a skylight (pages 56 to 59)
- Building a skylight shaft (pages 60 to 63)

### Everything You Need:

Tools: tape measure, level, pencil, combination square, reciprocating saw, flat pry bar, miter saw, hammer, ladders, roofing jacks, stapler, roofing knife, caulk gun, metal snips, plumb bob.

Materials: 2" dimension lumber, 10d nails, building paper, roofing cement, skylight flashings, roofing nails, insulation, twine, sheet plastic.

## Skylight Shaft Options

**Straight shafts** are easy to build, and work well if you prefer soft, diffuse natural lighting. The sides of the light shaft run straight down to the framed ceiling opening.

**Angled shafts** are longer at the base, allowing a greater amount of direct sunlight into a room. An angled shaft also is more effective for directing light toward a particular area of a room.

## Installation Variations

Trusses

**No light shaft is required** for skylights in finished attics where the ceiling surface is attached directly to rafters. Install the window low enough on the roof to provide a view of the surrounding landscape.

**Install several small skylights,** instead of one large one, if your home is framed with roof trusses instead of rafters. Each skylight must fit in the space between the roof trusses. Trusses are critical to the structural strength of the roof, and should never be cut or altered.

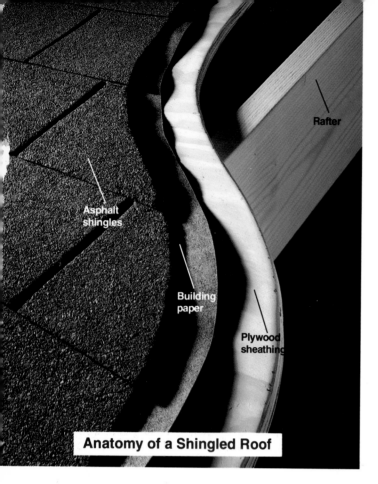

**Anatomy of a Shingled Roof**

Rafter

Asphalt shingles

Building paper

Plywood sheathing

## Removing a Shingled Roof Section

When installing a skylight, you will need to remove a section of roof. Asphalt or fiberglass shingles are easy to remove; but slate, tile, or wood-shingle roofs should be left to a professional.

Use extreme caution whenever you are working on a roof. Never work on a roof alone, and always wear long pants and rubber-soled shoes. Use metal roofing jacks and 2 × 10s to provide a foot rest below the work area (page opposite). If possible, start your roofing project on a calm, clear day when the temperature is between 50° and 70°F. Cold shingles are slippery from condensation, and warm shingles are easily damaged.

**Everything You Need:**

Tools: ladder, hammer, chalk line, tape measure, roofing jacks, circular saw with old remodeler's blade.

Materials: 8d casing nails, 2 × 4, straight 1 × 4, roofing cement.

## How to Remove a Shingled Roof Section

**1** After framing the rough opening from the inside (pages 56 to 57), mark the rough opening by driving 8d casing nails through the interior roof sheathing at the corners of the frame.

**2** Nail a 2 × 4 diagonally across the framed opening to keep the roof section from falling through when it is cut loose.

Work area

Roofing jack below work area

Roofing jack at roof edge

**3** Attach a pair of roofing jacks just above the roof edge, and attach another pair just below the work area. Lay 2"- thick planks across each pair of jacks.

**4** Measure between the nails to make sure the rough opening dimensions are accurate. Snap chalk lines on the shingles between the nails to mark the rough opening. Drive nails back through roof.

**5** Use casing nails to attach a straight 1 × 4 flush along the inside edge of one cutting line. Use a nail set to drive the heads below the wood surface so they do not scratch the saw foot.

**6** Cut through the shingles and sheathing along the marked line, using a circular saw and remodeler's blade set to maximum depth. (Use an old saw blade, because mineral particles in shingles will ruin a new blade.) Rest the saw foot on the 1 × 4 to protect it from scratches, and use the edge of the board as a guide. Reposition the 1 × 4 and cut along the remaining lines. **Do not stand or lean on the cutout area.**

**7** After the cut section drops down onto the diagonal 2 × 4 brace, carefully lift it out of the hole. Remove the diagonal brace and continue with the skylight installation (pages 52 to 63). When the job is done, remove the roofing jacks, and fill the nail holes with roofing cement.

## How to Install a Skylight

**1** Prepare the project area by removing any insulation between the joists or rafters. (In a finished attic, you will need to expose the rafters by removing the interior surfaces.)

**2** Use the first rafter on each side of the planned rough opening to serve as king rafters. Measure and mark where the double header and double sill will fit against one of the king rafters. Use a carpenter's level to extend the marks across the intermediate rafter to the opposite king rafter.

**3** Brace each intermediate rafter by nailing two 2 × 4s between the rafter and the joist below. Braces should be positioned just above the header marks and just below the sill marks.

**4** Reinforce each king rafter by attaching a full-length "sister" rafter against the outside edge, using 10d nails. Use a combination square to mark the section of intermediate rafter that will be removed. To accommodate the double header and sill, the removed section of rafter should be 6" longer than the listed rough opening height of the skylight.

**5** Remove the intermediate rafter by cutting along the marked lines, using a reciprocating saw. Make an additional cut about 3" inside the first cut, then knock out the small rafter section. Pry out the remaining section of cut rafter with a pry bar.

**6** Build a double header and double sill to reach between the king rafters, using 2" dimension lumber that is the same size as the rafters.

**7** Install the header and sill, anchoring them to the king rafters and cripple rafters with 10d nails. The ends of the header and sill should be aligned with the marked lines on the king rafters.

**8** Measure and mark the rough opening width on the header and sill. For some skylight sizes, this measurement will equal the distance between the king rafters. If the measurement is less than the distance between king rafters, trimmers need to be installed.

**9** Cut and install trimmers to complete the skylight frame. Inside edges of trimmers should just touch the rough opening width marks on the header and sill. Avoid installing trimmers by using rafters and joists to frame the opening whenever possible.

**10** Remove the 2 × 4 braces supporting the cripple rafters, then mark the rough opening, and cut and remove the roof section as directed on pages 54 to 55.

**11** Remove shingles around the rough opening with a flat pry bar, exposing at least 9" of building paper or sheathing on all sides of the roof opening. Remove entire shingles only; do not cut them.

(continued next page)

**12** Cut 1-ft.-wide strips of building paper and slide them between the shingles and existing building paper or sheathing. Bend the paper around the framing members and staple it in place.

Nailing flange

Roofing cement

**13** Spread a 5"-wide layer of roofing cement around the rough opening. Insert the skylight in the rough opening so the nailing flange rests tightly against the building paper.

**14** Nail through the nailing flange and into the framing members with 2" galvanized roofing nails spaced every 6". (NOTE: If your skylight uses L-shaped brackets instead of a nailing flange, follow the manufacturer's instructions.)

Adhesive strip

**15** Patch in shingles up to the bottom edge of the skylight. Attach the shingles with roofing nails driven just below the adhesive strip. (If necessary, cut the shingles with a roofing knife to make them fit against the bottom of the skylight.)

Skylight jamb

Side flange

**16** Spread roofing cement on the bottom edge of the sill flashing, then fit the flashing around the bottom of the skylight unit. Attach the flashing by driving 3/4" galvanized nails through the vertical side flanges near the top of the flashing and into the skylight jambs.

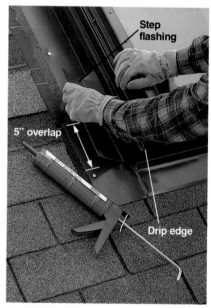

Step flashing

5" overlap

Drip edge

**17** Spread roofing cement on the bottom of a piece of step flashing, then slide the flashing under the drip edge on one side of the skylight. Step flashing should overlap the sill (bottom) flashing by 5". Press the step flashing down to bond it. Repeat at the opposite side of the skylight.

**18** Patch in next row of shingles on each side of the skylight, following the existing shingle pattern. Drive a roofing nail through each shingle and the step flashing, into the sheathing. Drive additional nails just above the notches in the shingles.

**19** Continue applying alternate layers of step flashing and shingles, using roofing cement and roofing nails. Each flashing should overlap the preceding flashing by 5".

**20** At the top of the skylight, cut and bend the last step flashing on each side, so the vertical flange wraps around the corner of the skylight. Patch in the next row of shingles.

**21** Spread roofing cement on the bottom of the head flashing to bond it to the roof. Position the flashing against the top of the skylight so the vertical flange fits under the skylight drip edge, and the horizontal flange fits under the shingles above the skylight.

**22** Fill in the remaining shingles, cutting them to fit, if necessary. Attach the shingles with roofing nails driven just above the notches.

**23** Apply a complete bead of roofing cement along the joint between the shingles and skylight. Remove roofing jacks and fill nail holes with roofing cement.

## How to Build a Skylight Shaft

**1** Remove any insulation in the area where the ceiling opening will be located. If there is electrical wiring running through the project area, shut off the power and reroute the circuit before continuing.

**2** Using a plumb bob as a guide, mark reference points on the ceiling surface, directly below the inside corners of the skylight frame. If you are installing a straight shaft, these points will mark the corners of the ceiling opening.

Plumb mark

**3** If the skylight shaft will be angled, measure from the plumb marks and mark the corners of the ceiling opening. Drive finish nails through the ceiling surface to mark the points.

**4** From the room below, mark lines between the finish nails, then remove the ceiling surface.

**5** Use one joist on each side of the ceiling opening to serve as king joists. Measure and mark where the double header and double sill will fit against the king joists, and where the outside edge of the header and sill will cross any intermediate joists.

**6** If you will be removing a section of an intermediate joist, reinforce the king joists by nailing full-length "sister" joists to the outside edge of the king joists, using 10d nails.

**7** Use a combination square to extend cutting lines down the sides of the intermediate joist, then cut out the joist section with a reciprocating saw. Pry the joist loose, being careful not to damage ceiling surface.

**8** Build a double header and double sill to span the distance between the king joists, using 2" dimension lumber the same size as the joists.

(continued next page)

**9** Install the double header and double sill, anchoring them to the king joists and cripple joists with 10d nails. The inside edges of the header and sill should be aligned with the edge of the ceiling cutout.

**10** Complete the ceiling opening by cutting and attaching trimmers, if required, along the sides of the ceiling cutout between the header and sill. End-nail the trimmers to the header and sill with 10d nails.

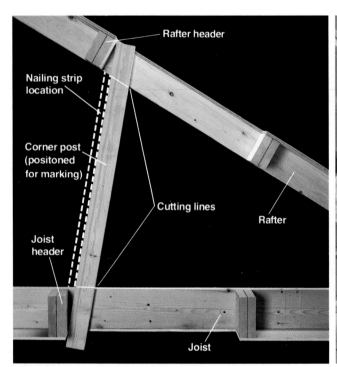

**11** Install 2 × 4 corner posts for the skylight shaft. To measure posts, begin with a 2 × 4 that is long enough to reach from the top to the bottom of the shaft. Hold the 2 × 4 against the inside of the framed openings, so it is flush with the top of the rafter header and the bottom of the joist header

(left). Mark cutting lines where the 2 × 4 meets the top of the joist or trimmer, and the bottom of the rafter or trimmer (right). Cut along the lines, then toenail the posts to the top and bottom of the frame with 10d nails.

**12** Attach a 2 × 4 nailing strip to the outside edge of each corner post to provide a surface for attaching wallboard. Ends of nailing strips should be notched to fit around the trimmers, but a perfect fit is not necessary.

**13** Install additional 2 × 4 nailing strips between posts if the distances between corners posts is more than 24". The top ends of the nailing strips should be mitered to fit against the rafter trimmers.

**14** Wrap the skylight shaft with fiberglass insulation. Secure the insulation by wrapping twine or duct tape around the shaft and insulation.

**15** From inside the shaft, staple a plastic vapor barrier over the insulation.

**16** Finish the inside of the shaft using metal corner beads and wallboard. TIP: To reflect light, paint shaft interior with light semi-gloss paint.

# Repairing Siding & Trim

The materials we use to cover the outside of our home have changed dramatically in recent years. But even with the advances, one fact has not changed: all types of siding and trim need some maintenance or repair from time to time.

Traditional wood lap siding can be repaired quite easily if, like most homeowners, you have some experience repairing wood. Epoxy-based wood fillers and long-lasting caulk products make the task easy. And replacing missing or damaged wood shakes is one of the simplest exterior home repairs.

Repairing masonry siding, like brick veneer and stucco, no longer requires a skilled mason. It can be repaired with a few easy-to-apply products.

But perhaps the most significant change in siding maintenance and repair has come with "low-maintenance" or "no-maintenance" manufactured siding products. Once viewed as gimmicks sold door-to-door, aluminum, vinyl, and steel siding products have become commonplace in the past few decades. When they first hit the market, repair of these products was the exclusive terrain of licensed contractors, but now most building centers carry a range of replacement parts and repair products. As a result, simple repairs can be done by do-it-yourselfers.

However, there are still some repairs you should think twice about attempting. If the damage to your siding (whatever its type) is so extensive that it appears to require full replacement, you should consider hiring a contractor. Few home improvement projects are more time-consuming than applying new siding—especially if you are installing products that you have never worked with before. There is a lot of competition among siding contractors, and you can usually come up with a range of bids. But do not look only at the cost—whenever hiring a contractor, check references and licenses, and get estimates in writing.

This section shows:

# Evaluating Siding & Trim

**Siding damage,** like the water damage caused by the leaky hose bib shown above, often requires replacement of the affected siding pieces. Identify and eliminate the cause of the damage before you replace or repair siding and trim.

The first step in inspecting and evaluating siding and trim is to identify with certainty the material types (photos, below). Once you have determined the material, take a closer look for any potential problems (photos, right). If your siding is under warranty, read the warranty document closely before attempting any repairs. Making repairs yourself could invalidate the product warranty.

**CAUTION:** many homes built in the 1940s and 1950s were covered with milled asbestos shingles. Asbestos shingles have the same general appearance as fiberglass, usually with a rough, heavily ridged surface. Because asbestos is classified as a hazardous material, its handling and disposal are regulated. Contact your local waste management department before handling asbestos shingles.

## Common Siding Types

**Wood lap siding** is usually made of cedar, pine, or hardwood particle board. Beveled boards are the most common. Wood lap is very easy to repair (pages 70 to 72).

**Shakes & shingles:** Shakes (shown) and shingles usually are cut from cedar or pine. Basic repairs are easy on wood shakes and shingles (page 72).

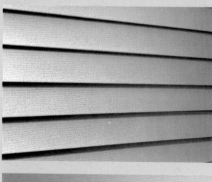

**Vinyl siding** is virtually maintenance-free. Minor repairs can be made with caulk or patches (pages 74 to 75). Contact a siding contractor before making major repairs.

**Brick:** Small problems in brick veneer can be repaired with quick-fix concrete repair products. For major repairs, contact an expert.

**Metal siding:** Minor patching and caulking can take care of many common problems affecting metal siding (pages 74 to 75). Contact a contractor for major repairs.

**Stucco:** Minor repairs, like filling thin cracks or small holes, can be made with concrete or stucco repair products (page 73). For wide cracks and major damage, call an expert.

## Common Siding Problems

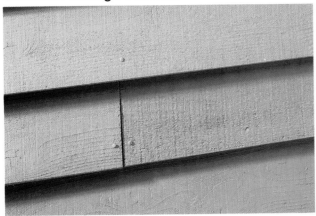

**Separated joints** can occur in any type of lap siding, but are most common in wood lap. Gaps between ⅛" and ¼" thick can be filled with caulk. Gaps ⅜" or wider could mean that your house has a serious moisture or shifting problem: consult a professional inspector.

**Buckling** occurs most frequently in manufactured siding, when expansion gaps are too small at the points where the siding fits into trim and channels. If possible, move the channel slightly. If not, remove the siding (page 72), trim length slightly, then reinstall.

**Minor surface damage** to metal siding is best left alone in most cases—unless damage has penetrated the surface (page 69). With metal products, cosmetic surface repairs often look worse than the damage.

**Missing siding,** like the cedar shakes that have been blown from the wall shown above, should be replaced immediately (pages 68 to 75). Check the surrounding siding to make sure it is secure.

## Tips for Inspecting Trim

**Check window and door trim** for rot, especially on horizontal surfaces and at joints. Try to make repairs without removal (pages 76 to 77).

**Remove decorative trim,** like the gingerbread trim above, if you suspect damage. Inspecting and repairing it is easier in a workshop.

**Evaluate broad trim pieces,** like the end cap trim shown above, and make repairs using the same techniques used for siding.

**Stagger vertical seams** to make your siding repairs less visible. Where possible, drive fasteners into framing members. Siding sheathing or underlayment, if present at all, is often made from soft composite boards that do not hold fasteners well.

# Repairing Siding

Repairing common types of siding damage is a manageable project for most homeowners. Small to medium-size holes, cracks, and rotted areas can be repaired by filling with repair products or by replacing the damaged sections with matching siding.

As with most exterior repair projects, the primary goal of siding repair is to make sure minor or moderate damage does not turn into major damage. But a well-executed siding repair also will add to the visual appeal of your home, especially if the repair materials are a good blend with the surrounding siding.

If you cannot find new matching siding for patches at building centers, check with salvage yards or siding contractors. When repairing aluminum or vinyl siding, contact the manufacturer or the contractor who installed the siding to help you locate matching materials and parts. If you cannot find an exact match, remove original siding from a less-visible area of your house, like the back of the garage, and use it as the patch. Patch the gap in the less-visible area with the near-match siding.

## Tips for Repairing Siding

**Create an expansion gap** at each seam between wood siding panels or lap siding. Use a nail as a guide to set the width of the gaps (for most siding types, ⅛" is an adequate expansion gap). Fill the gaps with exterior caulk.

**Repair small holes** with the appropriate filler product. For *wood siding* (top), fill holes with epoxy wood filler. Paint to match. For *metal and vinyl siding* (bottom), use tinted exterior caulk to fill holes. If you cannot find a matching color at a building center, check with the siding manufacturer.

**Number the siding pieces** as you remove them from your house to simplify reinstallation. You can also use the boards as templates for replacement pieces.

**Patch damaged building paper** before attaching new siding. When applying a patch, loosen the building paper above the damaged area, and slip the top of the patch underneath. Attach the patch with staples. Use roof cement to patch small holes or tears.

**Insert spacers** between the siding and sheathing above the work area while you make repairs to lap siding. This creates better access, simplifying the repair process. **CAUTION:** Metal siding will buckle if bent too far.

## Repairing Wood Siding

Wood siding is the easiest type to repair. Fixing cracks, replacing damaged sections, and filling holes requires only basic carpentry tools and inexpensive materials. Only use wood and wood repair products that are suitable for exterior use.

### Everything You Need:

Tools: hammer, chisel, trowel, screwdrivers, hacksaw, circular saw, keyhole saw, pry bar, nail set, electronic stud finder, paint brush.

Materials: epoxy wood filler, epoxy glue, nails and deck screws, siliconized acrylic caulk, plastic roof cement, building paper, lumber crayon, sheathing, wood preservative, primer, paint or stain.

**Repair cracks and splits** in wood siding with epoxy wood glue. Apply the glue to both sides of the crack, then press the board back together. For best results, position a board under the bottom edge of the damaged board and press it upward to create even pressure until the glue sets (if working near the ground, wedge a 2 × 4 under the board). After the glue sets, drive galvanized deck screws on each side of the crack to reinforce the repair. Clean off excess glue, and touch up the repair with paint.

## How to Replace a Section of Wood Lap Siding

**1** Using an electronic stud finder, locate and mark framing members around the repair area. Mark cutout lines over the centers of framing members on each side of the repair area. Stagger the lines so vertical joints do not align (page 68, top photo).

**2** Insert spacers beneath the board above the repair area. Make entry cuts at the tops of the cutting lines with a keyhole saw, then saw through the boards with the saw in an upright position. Remove the boards. Pry out any nails, or cut off the heads with a hacksaw blade.

**TIP:** Trace cutouts for any fixtures, wall openings, or other obstructions using the old siding board as a template. Also mark the end lines if the template board is still intact (make sure there will be a ⅛"-wide expansion gap at each end). Make the cutouts with a jig saw or coping saw, then cut to length.

**3** Measure and cut all replacement siding boards to fit, leaving an expansion gap of ⅛" at each end. Apply wood preservative/sealer or primer to the ends and back sides of the boards before installation.

**4** Nail the new boards in place with ring-shank siding nails, starting with the lowest board. Drive nails into framing members using the original nailing pattern (normally at 12" intervals through the bottom of the exposed board and the top of the board below).

**5** Fill expansion joints with caulk (use paintable caulk for painted wood, and tinted caulk for stained wood), then prime and paint or stain the replacement siding boards to match the surrounding boards.

# How to Replace Wood Shakes & Shingles

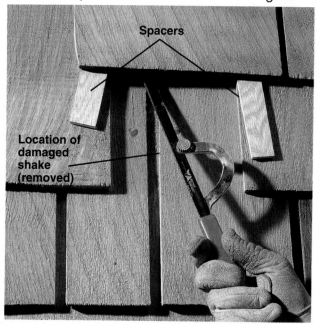

**1** Split damaged shakes or shingles with a hammer and chisel, and remove. Insert wood spacers under the shakes or shingles above the repair area, then slip a hacksaw blade under the top board to cut off any nail heads remaining from the old shake or shingle.

**2** Cut replacement shakes or shingles to fit, leaving a ⅛" to ¼"-wide expansion gap at each side. Coat all sides and edges with wood preservative. Slip the patch pieces under the siding above the repair area (start on lower courses if patching a large area). Attach with ring-shank siding nails, driven near the top of the exposed area on the patch. Cover nail heads with caulk, wiping off any excess. Remove spacers.

# How to Replace Siding Panels

**1** Remove battens or trim securing the damaged panels. Pry out the entire damaged panel. Inspect the building paper under the panels, and patch as needed.

**2** Cut replacement panels from matching material, allowing a ⅛"-wide expansion gap at side seams. Prime or seal the edges and back side of the replacement boards before installing.

**3** Nail the new boards in place with ring-shank siding nails. Caulk all seams and expansion joints, then replace battens and other trim. Prime and paint or stain to match.

# Repairing Stucco

Stucco is a very long-lasting siding product. But, over time, it will crumble and crack. Making permanent repairs to extensively damaged stucco walls is a job for a professional, but most homeowners can make smaller repairs with simple repair products.

Use premixed stucco repair compound for patching small holes or crumbled areas in stucco walls. Use concrete or stucco repair caulk for filling small cracks.

## Everything You Need:

Tools: wire brush, putty knife, whisk broom.

Materials: concrete caulk, stucco repair compound.

**Fill thin cracks** with concrete caulk. Overfill the crack with caulk, and feather until it is flush with the stucco. Allow the caulk to set, then paint to match. Concrete caulk stays semiflexible, preventing further cracking.

## How to Patch Stucco Walls

**1** Clean out loose material from the repair area with a wire brush. Remove rust from any exposed metal lath, and treat the lath with metal primer.

**2** Trowel premixed stucco repair compound into the repair area with a putty knife or pointed trowel, overfilling slightly (read manufacturer's directions—drying times and application techniques vary).

**3** Smooth out the repair with a putty knife or trowel, feathering it even with the surrounding surface. Use a whisk broom to create a matching texture on the stucco patch. Touch up with masonry paint to blend in the repair.

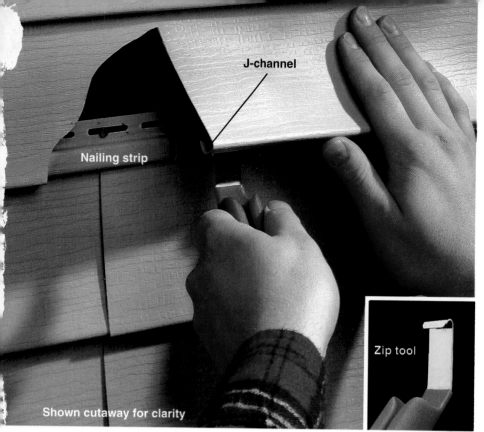

J-channel

Nailing strip

Zip tool

Shown cutaway for clarity

**Vinyl and metal siding pieces** have a locking J-channel that fits over the bottom of the nailing strip on the piece below. Use a zip tool (inset) to separate siding panels. Insert the zip tool at the overlapping seam nearest the repair area. Slide the zip tool over the J-channel, pulling outward slightly, to unlock the joint from the siding below.

# Repairing Vinyl & Metal Siding

Vinyl and metal siding are popular with homeowners because they are inexpensive and can last for decades. However, the materials are susceptible to dents, holes, and fading. Minor repairs can be done by do-it-yourselfers. For major work, and to help find replacement parts, contact the contractor that installed your siding, or the siding manufacturer.

## Everything You Need:

Tools: hammer, tape measure, drill, aviator snips, utility knife, caulk gun, zip tool, pry bar, straightedge.

Materials: nails; caulk; roof cement or exterior panel adhesive; end caps, trim, and siding panels as needed.

## How to Patch Vinyl Siding

Nailing strip trimmed off at overlap

Replacement piece

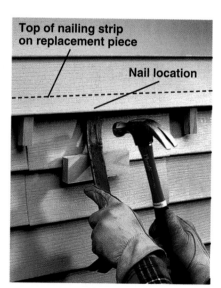

Top of nailing strip on replacement piece

Nail location

**1** Unlock interlocking joints with the siding above the repair area, using a zip tool (photo above). Start unlocking at the seam nearest the damaged area. Install spacers below the piece above, then pry out fasteners in the top piece of damaged siding, using a flat pry bar.

**2** Cut out the damaged area, using a straightedge and utility knife; then cut a replacement piece 4" longer than the open area, from similar siding material. Before installing, trim off 2" of the nailing strip from each end of the replacement piece in the overlap area. Slide the piece into position.

**3** Attach the replacement siding. Because the nailing strip is difficult to reach with a hammer, press ring-shank siding nails in the slots of the nailing strip, then position the end of a flat pry bar over each nail head. Drive nails by rapping on the neck of the pry bar with a hammer. Slip the J-channel over the nailing strip (photo, top left).

## How to Patch Metal Siding

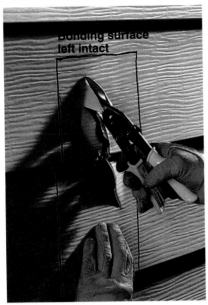

**1** Cut out the damaged area with aviator snips and a hacksaw blade. Leave some exposed surface area at the top of the uppermost piece you remove to serve as a bonding surface for the top siding patch.

**2** Cut a patch or patches 4" wider than the repair area, using matching material. Cut off the nailing strip from the top of the top patch piece. Make sure all edges are smooth, deburring with metal sandpaper if necessary.

**3** Nail lower patches in place by driving ring-shank siding nails through the nailing strips, starting with the lowest piece. To install the top piece, apply roof cement to the back, and press the patch in place, slipping the J-shaped locking channel over the nailing strip below. Caulk the seams.

## How to Replace Aluminum End Caps

**1** Remove the damaged end cap. If end caps cannot be removed easily, pry the bottom loose, then cut along the top with a hacksaw.

**2** Attach replacement end caps, starting at the bottom. Drive ring-shank siding nails through the nailing tabs, and into framing members.

**3** Trim the nailing tabs off the top replacement cap, then apply roof cement to the back. Snap the cap over the J-shaped locking channels of the siding courses. Press the top cap securely in place.

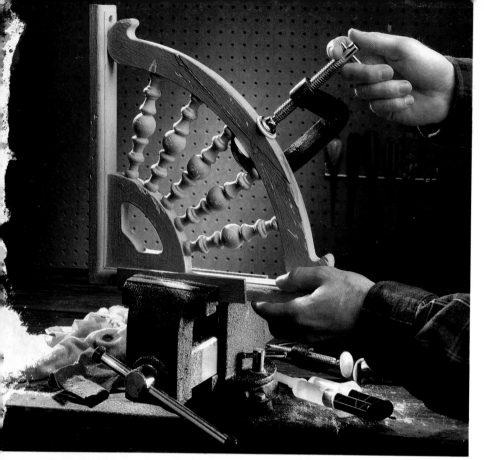

# Repairing Trim

Some exterior trim serves as decoration, like gingerbread and ornate cornice moldings. Other trim, like brick molding and end caps, works with siding to seal your house from the elements. Damaged brick molding and corner boards should be patched with stock material similar to the original. If you cannot find matching replacement parts for decorative trim, check salvage shops or contact a custom millworker.

**Everything You Need:**

Tools: hammer, chisel, circular saw, nail set, putty knife, utility knife, paint brush, flat pry bar.

Materials: epoxy wood filler, epoxy glue, caulk, nails and screws, sandpaper, paint, building paper, drip edge.

**Repair delicate or ornamental trim molding** in your workshop. You will get better results more easily than if you try repairing it while it is still attached. Leave decorative trim in place if you must remove siding to gain access to it.

## Tips for Repairing & Replacing Trim

**Reattach loose trim** with new ring-shank siding nails driven near old nail locations. Fill old nail holes with paintable caulk, and touch up caulk and new nail heads with paint to match the surrounding surface.

**Repair decorative trim molding** with epoxy glue or wood filler. For major repairs, make your own replacement parts, or take the trim to a custom millwork shop.

## How to Replace Brick Molding

**1** Pry off old brick molding around windows and doors using a flat pry bar. Remove any old drip edge. Inspect and repair the building paper (page 69). NOTE: Drip edge that fits above doors and windows is a different product from roof-style drip edge (page 15).

**2** Hold a replacement piece of brick molding, slightly longer than the original piece, across the opening. Mark cutting lines to fit the opening. Cut the replacement brick molding at the cutting lines, matching any miter cuts.

**3** Cut a 3"-wide piece of flashing to fit between the jambs, then bend it in half lengthwise to form the new drip edge (preformed drip edge is available). Slip it between the siding and the building paper, above the door or window. Do not nail the drip edge in place.

**4** Test-fit the replacement piece of brick molding, then apply exterior-grade panel adhesive to the back side. Follow the manufacturer's directions for allowing the adhesive to set.

**5** Nail the brick molding to the door header with 10d galvanized casing nails. Lock-nail the miter joints, and set all nail heads. Seal joints, and cover nail holes with caulk. Prime and paint when the caulk dries.

# Index

Cowles Creative Publishing, Inc.
offers a variety of how-to books.
For information write:
  Cowles Creative Publishing
  Subscriber Books
  5900 Green Oak Drive
  Minnetonka, MN 55343